Patriarca (Raymond) v. U.S. U.S. Supreme Court Transcript of Record with Supporting Pleadings

FRANCIS J DIMENTO, ERWIN N GRISWOLD, FRANCIS J DIMENTO

Patriarca (Raymond) v. U.S.
Petition / FRANCIS J DIMENTO / 1968 / 725 / 393 U.S. 1022 / 89 S.Ct. 633 / 21 L.Ed.2d 567 / 11-12-1968
Patriarca (Raymond) v. U.S.
Brief in Opposition (P) / ERWIN N GRISWOLD / 1968 / 725 / 393 U.S. 1022 / 89 S.Ct. 633 / 21 L.Ed.2d 567 / 12-12-1968
Patriarca (Raymond) v. U.S.
Petition for Rehearing / FRANCIS J DIMENTO / 1968 / 725 / 393 U.S. 1022 / 89 S.Ct. 633 / 21 L.Ed.2d 567 / 2-7-1969

Patriarca (Raymond) v. U.S. U.S. Supreme Court
Transcript of Record with Supporting Pleadings

Table of Contents

I. Petition

II. Brief in Opposition (P)

III. Petition for Rehearing

669

In the

Supreme Court of the United States

OCTOBER TERM, 1968

No. 725

RAYMOND PATRIARCA, RONALD J. CASSESSO
and HENRY TAMELEO,

PETITIONERS,

v.

UNITED STATES OF AMERICA,

RESPONDENT.

PETITION FOR A WRIT OF CERTIORARI TO THE UNITED STATES COURT OF APPEALS FOR THE FIRST CIRCUIT

FRANCIS J. DIMENTO
100 State Street
Boston, Massachusetts 02109
Tel: (617) 523-5253
Attorney for Petitioner Patriarca

RONALD J. CHISHOLM
261 Tremont Street
Boston, Massachusetts 02116
Tel: (617) 426-8688
Attorney for Petitioner Cassesso

JOSEPH J. BALLIRO
44 School Street
Boston, Massachusetts 02108
Tel: (617) 227-5822
Attorney for Petitioner Tameleo

Blanchard Press, Inc., Boston, Mass. — Law Printers

TABLE OF CONTENTS

		Page
Opinion Below		2
Judgments Below		2
Jurisdiction		2
Questions Presented		2
Statutes Involved		3
Statement of the Case		4
	A. Proceedings Below	4
	B. The Pre-trial Publicity	6
	C. Substantive Trial Testimony	10
	D. Adjective Trial Testimony	11
	E. Government's Summation	13
Reasons for Granting the Writ		15
	I. Questions of broad importance to the administration of criminal justice in the federal courts are presented	15
	A. Prejudicial pre-trial publicity	15
	B. Improper Argument by Government Counsel	17
	C. The sufficiency of the evidence to establish an "attempt"	24
Conclusion		24
Appendix A		1a
Appendix B		19a

TABLE OF CITATIONS

Cases

Berger v. *United States*, 295 U.S. 78 (1935) 19

Delaney v. *United States*, 199 F.2d 107 (1st Cir. 1952) 16

Downum v. *United States*, 372 U.S. 734 (1963) 20

Page

Fleming v. United States, 332 F.2d 23 (1st Cir. 1964) 20

Greenberg v. United States, 280 F.2d 472 (1st Cir. 1960) 18

Harris v. United States, D.C. Cir. 9/17/68 21

Irvin v. Dowd, 366 U.S. 717 (1961) 15

Janko v. United States, 366 U.S. 716 (1961) 16

Kitchell v. United States, 354 F.2d 715 (1st Cir. 1966) 20

Lawn v. United States, 355 U.S. 339 (1958) 18

Marshall v. United States, 360 U.S. 310 (1959) 16

Rideau v. Louisiana, 373 U.S. 723 (1963) 15

Sheppard v. Maxwell, 384 U.S. 333 (1966) 15

Swift v. United States, 196 U.S. 375 (1905) 24

United States v. Bentvena, 319 F.2d 916 (2d Cir. 1963) 24

United States ex rel. Bloeth v. Denno, 313 F.2d 364 (2d Cir. 1963) 16

United States v. Kum Seng Seo, 300 F.2d 623 (3rd Cir. 1962) 16

United States v. Medlin, 353 F.2d 789 (6th Cir. 1965) 18

United States v. Socony-Vacuum Oil Co., 310 U.S. 239 (1940) 19

Statutes

18 U.S.C. 371 3

          1952 .... 3, 5

28 U.S.C. 1254(1) 2

In the
Supreme Court of the United States

OCTOBER TERM, 1968

No.

RAYMOND PATRIARCA, RONALD J. CASSESSO and HENRY TAMELEO,

PETITIONERS,

v.

UNITED STATES OF AMERICA,

RESPONDENT.

PETITION FOR A WRIT OF CERTIORARI TO THE UNITED STATES COURT OF APPEALS FOR THE FIRST CIRCUIT

Petitioners pray that a writ of certiorari issue to review the judgments of the United States Court of Appeals for the First Circuit entered in the above-entitled cases on October 14, 1968.

The petitioners file herewith a single petition in accordance with Rule 23 (5), their appeals in the lower court having been heard on a printed consolidated record appendix.[1]

---

[1] The letters "P.R." refer to Vol. I of petitioners' (appellants below) consolidated record appendix, containing the "Pleadings Record".

The letters "T.T." refer to Vols. II and III, containing the "Trial Transcript".

The letters "E.R." refer to Vol. IV, containing the "Exhibits Record".

Opinion Below

The opinion of the Court of Appeals for the First Circuit is not yet reported, but is annexed hereto as Appendix A.

Judgments Below

The judgments of the United States District Court for the District of Massachusetts were entered on April 9, 1968 (P.R. 22) and are printed at P.R. 45-50.

The judgments of the Court of Appeals for the First Circuit were entered on October 14, 1968, and are annexed hereto as Appendix B.

Jurisdiction

The judgments sought to be reviewed are dated, and were entered, October 14, 1968.

The jurisdiction of this Court is invoked pursuant to the provisions of 28 U.S.C. 1254 (1) and Rule 22 (2).

Questions Presented

1. (a) Should motions for continuance or change of venue have been granted where an attempt on the life of the attorney for the chief prosecution witness occurred only 34 days before commencement of trial and precipitated a barrage of prejudicial publicity which fed the public suspicion that the defendants were the culprits?

   (b) Should the additional publicity generated by good-faith motions for continuance or change of venue be disregarded in assessing the prejudice to defendants?

2. 9 (a) Was it error to permit Government counsel to argue in effect that disbelief by the jury of the only witness to the *corpus delicti*, whose credibility was the sole issue in the case, was the equivalent of calling the prosecuting attorney and investigative agency perjurers?

(b) Does the fact that the argument was repeated after being struck by the court on the first occasion require entry of judgments of acquittal where an immediate corrective instruction was forestalled by Government counsel's denial that he had made the argument?

3. Is an *attempt* to perform an act of committing a crime of violence, within the meaning of 18 U.S.C. 1952, established merely by evidence that defendants pointed out to a hired killer the haunts of the intended victim?

Statutes Involved

18 U.S.C.A.

§ 371. *Conspiracy to commit offense or to defraud United States*

If two or more persons conspire either to commit any offense against the United States, or to defraud the United States, or any agency thereof in any manner or for any purpose, and one or more of such persons do any act to effect the object of the conspiracy, each shall be fined not more than $10,000 or imprisoned not more than five years, or both.

18 U.S.C.A.

§ 1952. *Interstate and foreign travel or transportation in aid of racketeering enterprises*

4

(a) Whoever travels in interstate or foreign commerce
or uses any facility in interstate or foreign commerce,
including the mail, with intent to—

(1) distribute the proceeds of any unlawful activity;
or
(2) commit any crime of violence to further any unlawful activity; or
(3) otherwise promote, manage, establish, carry on,
or facilitate the promotion, management, establishment, or carrying on, of any unlawful activity,

and thereafter performs or attempts to perform any of
the acts specified in subparagraphs (1), (2), and (3), shall
be fined not more than $10,000 or imprisoned for not more
than five years, or both.

(b) As used in this section "unlawful activity" means
(1) any business enterprise involving gambling, liquor on
which the Federal excise tax has not been paid, narcotics,
or prostitution offenses in violation of the laws of the
State in which they are committed or of the United States,
or (2) extortion, bribery, or arson in violation of the laws
of the State in which committed or of the United States.

Statement of the Case

A. *The Proceedings Below*

This is a petition seeking review of judgments of the
Court of Appeals for the First Circuit affirming judgments
of conviction of the District Court for the District of
Massachusetts.

The indictment, returned on June 20, 1967 (P.R. 2),
is in three counts. The first count charges that the three
defendants and one Joseph Baron (the Government's prin-

cipal witness) conspired to violate 18 U.S.C. §§1952(a)(2) and (3) with intent to commit murder to further an unlawful gambling enterprise. The second and third counts charge certain of the defendants with substantive violations of §1952(a)(2). (P.R. 22-27).

On January 30, 1968, an attempt was made on the life of John E. Fitzgerald, Jr., legal counsel to the Government's principal witness, Joseph Baron. Motions for continuance bottomed on the resulting publicity were thereupon filed by all three defendants (P.R. 34-37) and allowed by the trial court. By Order dated February 2, 1968, it continued trial until March 4, 1968. (P.R. 38).

On February 20, 1968 (P.R. 14, 15), a second motion for continuance, alleging a continuation of the same conditions of prejudice, was filed by each of the three defendants. (P.R. 38-39). On the same date (P.R. 15), the defendants also filed motions for change of venue to the Southern District of New York. (P.R. 40). After hearing, the trial court, on February 27, 1968, denied both motions. Its memorandum decision, dated February 27, noted that a prior motion for change of venue had been waived by all defendants on October 30, 1967; that, because of possible prejudicial publicity (prior to the Fitzgerald incident), trial had been delayed to February 5, 1968, and again delayed (after the Fitzgerald incident of January 30) to March 4, 1968; and that no prior motion for change of venue had ever been pressed. (P.R. 41-42).

On the morning of the date fixed for trial, March 4, 1968, the defendants again filed motions for continuance and change of venue, alleging worsened conditions of prejudice. (P.R. 18, 42-43). Relying on its memorandum of February 27, the trial court, after hearing, denied both motions. (T.T. 3-11).

On March 4, 1968, the case proceeded to trial and concluded on March 8 with verdicts of guilty as to each defendant on every count in which he was named. (P.R. 19).

B. *The Pre-Trial Publicity*

The motions for continuance and change of venue which are the subjects of this petition are those which were filed on February 20, 1968, and again on the morning of trial, March 4, 1968. They are bottomed on a long history of publicity, beginning with the widely publicized "Valachi hearings", so-called, of 1963, which named the defendant Patriarca as "Boss" of the New England "Cosa Nostra" or "Mafia" and the defendant Tameleo as one of his subordinates. It is a matter of common knowledge that the publicity, surrounding Patriarca, at least, multiplied and persisted uninterrupted down to May, 1967, when the Government disclosed, in connection with a tax-evasion prosecution in Rhode Island, unconnected with Patriarca, that his office in Providence had been "bugged" for three years and that both he and Tameleo had engaged in highly compromising conversations with others. See, *e.g.*, Boston Sunday Advertiser, May 21, 1967.[2] (E.R. 1a-2a).

Almost immediately thereafter, the public was afforded a preview of the instant indictment, which was about to be returned on June 20, 1967. News reports began to appear that a "Mafia strongarm man", Joseph (Barboza) Baron, was "singing" to the F.B.I. The reports were embellished with accounts of theretofore unsolved murders and Baron's desire to avenge those victims who were his friends. Explicit reference was made to Patriarca and the Mafia's connection with these murders, and the need for heavy security precautions against gangland retaliation was dwelt upon. See *e.g.*, Boston Record American, May 25, 1967; Boston Globe, May 26, 1967. (E.R. 4a-5a).

---

[2] The newspaper articles in evidence are merely representative. The full extent of the publicity had, as a matter of physical necessity, to be left to judicial notice.

Then, with the return of the instant indictment on June 20, and the arraignment of the defendants on June 26, 1967, the whole performance was repeated by the news media, but with the addition of statements by the United States Attorney that this marked the first instance of a Cosa Nostra insider turning state's evidence. See, *e.g.*, Boston Globe, June 22, 1967. (E.R. 15a).

The defendants Patriarca and Tameleo continued to make news in October, 1967, when, as a result of testimony by Baron before a state grand jury, Tameleo was indicted and arrested for complicity in the murder of Edward Deegan. See, *e.g.*, Boston Herald Traveler, October 27, 1967. (E.R. 20a).

Then, in January, 1968, the defendant Cassesso appeared in the forefront with the news that he was one of three indicted by a state grand jury for conspiracy to cause another falsely to confess to the Deegan murder. This served also to revive interest in Tameleo as one of those originally indicted for the murder. See, *e.g.*, Boston Globe, January 16, 1968. (E.R. 21a).

The final calamity struck on January 30, 1968, when Baron's attorney, John E. Fitzgerald, Jr., was nearly killed by a bomb wired to the ignition of his automobile. The public commotion that followed, as reported by the various media of news, made it devastatingly clear that the motive for the attempt on Fitzgerald's life was his representation of Baron, the "underworld informer". The reports were that Baron was "slated to make his second court appearance [3] to give state's evidence next Tuesday in Federal District Court here", Boston Globe, January

---

[3] His first court appearance had been in January, 1968, when he testified against Gennaro Angiulo and two others charged with first degree murder. That case had been the subject of a separate stream of publicity since the prior August and affected the appellants here to the extent that Angiulo was constantly referred to as Patriarca's chief lieutenant.

31, 1968 (E.R. 28a), and that "Fitzgerald was listed as a prospective witness in a racketeering prosecution scheduled to begin shortly in Federal Court here," but that the United States Attorney would "neither confirm nor deny" this. Boston Globe, February 1, 1968. (E.R. 45a).

With the trial scheduled to begin on Tuesday, February 6, 1968, the trial court, in the midst of the tumult, had no alternative but to grant the defendants' motion for continuance. By Order dated February 2, 1968, the trial was postponed to March 4, 1968. (P.R. 38). The news reports of the postponement served further to identify the murder attempt with the defendants. The Boston Herald Traveler of February 3, 1968, denied any responsibility for the postponement (E.R. 62a) and, on the following day, in a Sunday feature story, speculated whether Fitzgerald was actually scheduled to testify for the prosecution. (E.R. 72a).

The publicity continued without respite after the Order of postponement. The Governor, the state's Attorney General, the Senate President, members of the state legislature, local District Attorneys, spokesmen for the various state and municipal police agencies, lawyers, Bar Associations, and newspaper columnists and editorialists all variously joined in condemning the vicious deed, deploring the contempt it displayed for judges, juries, and other agencies of law enforcement, analyzing its motives and causes, urging a $50,000 reward for the capture of the culprit, praising Fitzgerald, reviewing his background and that of Baron, identifying Baron and Valachi as the only two major informers of the past ten years, promising action and calling for it from others, decrying inaction and placing blame for it elsewhere, having their pictures taken at Fitzgerald's bedside, quarreling over jurisdiction and calling for an end to the quarreling, providing security for Fitzgerald, his family, and a witness to the bombing, accusing one another of making political capital out of the incident, raising a fund to aid the Fitzgerald family, demanding intensified investigations of organized crime, announcing threats against the lives of the District Attorney of Middlesex County, a newspaperman, and Fitzgerald's law partner, and generally commenting on the great need for public action in combatting organized crime and its leaders, who, as the attempt on Fitzgerald's life demonstrates, pose a previously unrecognized threat to the safety of innocent people. (E.R. 73a-100a).

Finally, with the uproar still raging, on February 20, 1968, the defendants filed new motions for continuance, alleging a continuation of the same conditions of prejudice. (P.R. 14, 15, 38-39). At the same time, motions for a change of venue to the Southern District of New York were filed. (P.R. 15, 40). After hearing, both motions were denied. In a memorandum dated February 27, 1968, the trial judge, without mention of the bombing incident, interpreted the publicity as involving merely the Mafia or Cosa Nostra and concluded that such publicity was likely to continue indefinitely throughout the nation. (P.R. 41).

The motions, although heard *in camera*, and the trial court's memorandum decision denying them generated more publicity of their own in the week before trial. (E.R. 102a-104a). Included was a report that Marfeo was eventually slain a year later only "one block from Patriarca's office on July 13, 1966' (E.R. 103a), although the indictment did not allege, nor was any evidence adduced at trial, that the alleged conspiracy or attempt achieved its object. Included as well were references to the Mafia and Cosa Nostra. (E.R. 103a-104a).

Also in this interim period, only 3 days before trial, the press reported the appearance, before a state legislative committee, of Correction Commissioner John A. Gavin urging favorable action on a so-called "Barboza Protection Bill" (permitting transfer of prisoners to federal custody for protection from the underworld) and included in the same article references to the three defendants, their upcoming trial and the Fitzgerald bombing incident. (E.R. 105a).

Then, on the morning of trial, March 4, 1968, the defendants filed new motions for continuance and change of venue, alleging a continuation, and increase in tempo, of the publicity and bringing the record up to date. These motions were denied with a statement by the court that it was incorporating the same reasons as set forth in its memorandum of February 27, denying similar motions filed February 20, 1968. (T.T. 8).

C. Substantive Trial Testimony

A surveillance by the Rhode Island State and Providence police forces between January and March 3, 1965, disclosed that one William Marfeo was conducting an illegal dice game at the Veterans Social Club, located in the Federal Hill section of Providence, Rhode Island. (T.T. 35-41, 69-73). On March 3, 1965, a raid was mounted on the premises, gambling paraphernalia was seized, and those present, including Marfeo, were arrested. (T.T. 41-47, 73-75, 80-81, 90).

On March 4, 1965, a captain of the Providence Police asked the defendant Patriarca for assistance in persuading Marfeo to stop the dice game. (T.T. 331-332, 334).

In May, 1965, remodelling of the Social Club began, obviously to obstruct further police interference, and was followed by a resumption of the activities observed prior to the raid of March 3, 1965. (T.T. 92-95, 100-101).

Against the foregoing background, the Government's principal witness, Joseph Baron, born "Barboza" (T.T. 118), testified that, on a Monday in late June or early July,

1965, during the course of a telephone conversation between Boston and Providence, he was invited by Tameleo to come to Providence and to bring with him the defendant Cassesso. (T.T. 133-142).

On the next morning, a Tuesday, Baron and Cassesso drove from Boston to Providence, where they had a conversation with Patriarca and Tameleo. Patriarca stated that he wanted Baron and Cassesso to kill Marfeo because the latter's refusal to stop his illegal dice game was drawing heat (*i.e.*, intensification of law enforcement activity), thereby disrupting Patriarca's gambling enterprise, located in the same area. Baron and the defendant Cassesso agreed to do the killing without compensation. (T.T. 147-155). On the same day at Patriarca's suggestion, Tameleo pointed out to Baron and Cassesso two places frequented by Marfeo. (T.T. 155-160).

On the next morning, a Wednesday, Baron was told by Tameleo, and again by Patriarca, that the police had learned of Patriarca's dispute with Marfeo and that Patriarca therefore wanted further action postponed. (T.T. 164-167).

D. *Adjective Trial Testimony*

The cross-examination of Baron revealed a man who, by common consent (T.T. 208) and his own admission (T.T. 208-209), was a murderer for profit. He had a lengthy and serious criminal record (T.T. 257-263), had spent 16 of his 35 years in prison (T.T. 119-120), was then serving a state sentence of 4 to 5 years on various gun carrying charges (T.T. 118-119), had five or six state indictments still pending against him (T.T. 287), including one or more for being an habitual criminal (T.T. 201), and, in desperate expectation of serving an additional twelve to fifteen years (T.T. 192), had been planning to escape from prison and rejoin his paramour. (T.T. 216). Then, according to his testimony, at a time when he was very deeply concerned about his future (T.T. 187), he received an offer of "help" from agents of the FBI in exchange for his "help" (T.T. 200) and was thereafter transferred to another prison for "brainwashing." (T.T. 214). While in prison, he wrote to his paramour that he had "a few aces up his sleeve" (T.T. 216) and that "30 would go" whether "innocent or not". (T.T. 268). He was promised by the Government that his cooperation would be brought to the attention of the state courts in connection with the indictments pending against him[4] (T.T. 286-287) and that he would not be indicted in the instant matter. (T.T. 184-185, 311-312). Then, after giving his testimony before the grand jury which returned this indictment, he was transferred to federal custody and allowed to live with his wife (T.T. 281) and continue his illicit "loansharking" business. (T.T. 228-230). In the meantime, he had been negotiating to sell book and moving picture rights to the story of his exploits (T.T. 219-225), and had planned to avenge the deaths of his friends and the theft from them of some $70,000 intended for him. (T.T. 292-295).

The credibility of other Government witnesses, none of whom directly corroborated Baron, was not challenged on cross-examination. The only other adjective evidence was supplied by an agent of the FBI, Dennis Condon, who testified that he promised Baron that he would transmit to the United States Attorney Baron's fears for the safety of his wife and child and that the degree of Baron's cooperation would be made known to the state's District Attorney. He further testified that he heard the United States Attor-

---

[4] On November 1, 1968, Baron appeared in the Superior Court for Suffolk County with his attorney, John Fitzgerald, on these indictments, which were ordered "filed" indefinitely.

13

ney promise Baron that, if Baron cooperated, he would not be indicted. (T.T. 310-312).

E. *The Government's Summation*

With the evidence in this state and against the background of the pre-trial publicity heralding Baron as the great informer, the stage was set for jury summations built exclusively around the issue of the credibility of Baron, the Government's sole witness to the *corpus delicti*.

At the conclusion of arguments by defense counsel, the United States Attorney began his summation and, after one, short introductory paragraph, proceeded as follows (T.T. 497):

"At the outset I would like to comment briefly upon defense counsels' arguments.

"Basically all of them say that Joseph Baron and Joseph Baron's testimony is not fact, it's fiction. If you accept that, you also accept the fact that that fiction was written, produced and directed by the United States Attorney's office, by the Federal Bureau of Investigation, by the police in Revere and the police in Boston—

"Mr. Curran: I object.

"Mr. Chisholm: There is no such evidence. I object, your Honor.

"Mr. Balliro: That argument hasn't been made by the defense.

"The Court: Strike it out, please."

Then, after some nineteen more transcript pages of argument to the effect that Baron was in fact telling a credible story and was in fact corroborated by events testified to by other witnesses, the prosecutor continued to argue as follows (T.T. 516-517):

> "Did all this testimony from these people who way back to 1965 probably never heard of Joe Baron, all of a sudden just begin to fit together when Joe Baron decides he is going to testify?
>
> "I say that is an insult to your intelligence, and I also say that if Joe Baron is guilty of making it fiction, then I am guilty of making it fiction, and the FBI is guilty of making it fiction and every other witness who testified in this case is guilty of making up fiction.
>
> "Mr. Balliro: I object.
>
> "The Court: That may be argued."

The argument proceeded only for another page of the transcript and, immediately upon its conclusion, defense counsel orally moved at the bench for mistrial on the basis of the above-quoted portion (T.T. 521), which motion was denied (T.T. 523). The following colloquy occurred at the bench (T.T. 521-523):

> "Mr. Balliro: We move for a mistrial, based upon the grounds—
>
>   *   *   *
>
> "Mr. Balliro: It has to do with the government attorney identifying himself with Mr. Baron to the extent that if this jury believes Mr. Baron and feels he is a liar they also must feel the attorneys for the government and the officers—
>
> "The Court: Strike that out.
>
> "Mr. Balliro: It was left in the last time he argued it again.
>
> "Mr. Markham: I didn't say that.

"The Court: What was that?

"Mr. Balliro: We don't believe that Mr. Markham is a fabricator or anything of that sort. I have known him for a long time and I consider that he is a friend. I think it is prejudicial argument and it sort of puts Mr. Markham in the role of—

"The Court: It is trivial, Joe.

"Mr. Balliro: I think it is an effective argument.

"The Court: I ruled it out at one time when he put himself in the picture. He did it again. Did you do it again?

"Mr. Markham: No, Judge. I said if this is fiction, then every witness who appeared here is fiction.

"The Court: You weren't a witness. Did you put yourself in there?

"Mr. Markham: I asked a few leading questions on occasion, Judge.

"The Court: You all commit that error, but you can't help that. All lawyers do it.

"The motion for mistrial, Mr. Balliro, is denied.
    (Adjournment.)"

Reasons for Granting the Writ

I. QUESTIONS OF BROAD IMPORTANCE TO THE ADMINISTRATION OF CRIMINAL JUSTICE IN THE FEDERAL COURTS ARE PRESENTED.

A. *Prejudicial Pre-Trial Publicity*

In recent times there has been an increasing recognition that a new trial must be granted where prejudicial publicity has infected a trial and the court has not taken adequate measures to counteract it. *E.g., Sheppard v. Maxwell,* 384 U.S. 333 (1966); *Rideau v. Louisiana,* 373 U.S. 723 (1963); *Irvin v. Dowd,* 366 U.S. 717 (1961);

Janko v. United States, 366 U.S. 716 (1961); *Marshall v. United States*, 360 U.S. 310 (1959); *United States ex rel. Bloeth v. Denno*, 313 F.2d 364 (2d Cir. 1963); *United States v. Kum Seng Seo*, 300 F.2d 623, 624-626 (3rd Cir. 1962); *Delaney v. United States*, 199 F.2d 107 (1st Cir. 1952).

The initial issue, whether petitioners were prejudiced at all by the news of the bombing incident, may be quickly resolved by reference to the trial court's order of February 2 (P.R. 38), which, in granting a continuance to March 4, 1968, necessarily recognized the existence of the asserted prejudice. The simple truth is that, with the news of the bombing, all eyes in New England turned at once to the petitioners as the most likely culprits. It may be true, as the Court of Appeals suggests, that no report directly accused petitioners of responsibility for the bombing. It may also be true that an attempt to kill the chief prosecution witness's lawyer was not cited by the American Bar Association as presenting one of the "greatest hazards" to a fair trial (App. A, 6a). On the other hand, it surely cannot be the law that petitioners may be fairly convicted of crime by a jury which suspects them of resorting to murder in an attempt to avoid trial and conviction whereas, had the same jury been aware, for example, that petitioners refused "to submit to certain tests" (App. A, 6a), fairness would have required a new trial.

Apparently, it was the second issue, the adequacy of the 34-day delay between the bombing and the trial, on which the decision of the Court of Appeals turned. That Court concluded that, although the publicity continued right up to the day of trial (E.R. 106a), its volume was sufficiently reduced by that time to permit a fair trial.[5] In *Delaney*

---

[5] The last article to treat the petitioners, Baron and the bombing incident in a single package (leaving the necessary inferences to the reader) appeared three days before trial, on March 1, 1968 (E.R. 105a).

v. *United States*, 199 F.2d 107 (1st Cir. 1952), the same
Circuit had held inadequate a period of one month and
a half between trial and the one-shot publicity arising from
the account by a national magazine of a "scandal" involving the defendant. We do not, of course, suggest that this
Court lay down an objective time standard by which to
measure the dissipation of prejudice. On the other hand,
the apparent rule of the First Circuit here enunciated, that
virtually any lapse of time is sufficient so long as the
publicity has begun to subside before trial, seems wholly
unreasonable.

A third question, which is apparently entirely new, arises
from the appellate court's suggestion that publicity engendered by motions for delay and change of venue should be
excluded from consideration in assessing the quantum of
prejudice affecting the defendants. We submit that an
alternative rule would not mean that "cases would never
be tried", as the Court of Appeals suggests. (App. A, 5a).
Surely, some standards can be devised by this Court which
would guide the lower courts in determining the weight to
be given to publicity generated by defense motions. We
would suggest that, at the very least, the lower courts
should be required to consider whether the motion is color-
ably meritorious, whether brought in good faith, and
whether counsel has taken all reasonable steps, including
a request for a closed hearing, to avoid further publicity.
Without the intervention of this Court one can only
speculate as to how many meritorious motions for con-
tinuances or change of venue will be withheld in the future
solely because defense counsel are unwilling to risk the
consequences of failure.

B. *Improper Argument by Government Counsel*

The general rule in the lower Federal courts seems to be
that a prosecutor may express his personal belief as long

as he does not hint that such belief is supported by evidence known only to him. See *United States v. Medlin*, 353 F.2d 789, 796 (6th Cir. 1965). The First Circuit, in refusing to follow this rule, has condemned all statements of personal belief regardless of whether they hint of secret evidence. See *Greenberg v. United States*, 280 F.2d 472, 475 (1st Cir. 1960). This Court, on the other hand, in a situation where the asserted impropriety was invited and not objected to, seems to have approved the general rule. *Lawn v. United States*, 355 U.S. 339, 359, fn. 15 (1958).

In the instant case, the Court of Appeals found that the prosecutor's argument "was a back-handed way of laying one's credibility on the line" to support a case which "depended wholly on the credibility of" (App. A, 14a) one man, who "was a highly vulnerable witness" (App. A, 9a), but that the error was harmless because "all of the many factors which made [Baron's testimony] susceptible to impeachment were fully presented and fully argued" (App. A, 15a) and because defense counsel did not press its objection to the point of suggesting that the allegedly improper portion of the argument be read back to the trial court by the reporter.

That the entire case depended on the credibility of a single, highly vulnerable witness was precisely the point of the petitioners' objection below. The one vital piece of evidence lacking in the Government's case was direct corroboration of Baron. In their summations, defense counsel had directed their entire attack against Baron's credibility and the lack of evidence directly corroborating him. All that the Government's case lacked to tip the scales, if not already askew because of the jury's suspicions concerning petitioners' responsibility for the bombing,[6] was some

_____

[6] Petitioners submit that the prejudicial publicity cannot be separated from the improper argument and that the two issues should be considered together in assessing the total prejudice to petitioners in what

indication that Baron did not stand alone. This critical deficiency was supplied by the prosecutor's statement of personal belief, which, rather than being submerged in the extensive arguments of all counsel directed toward the evidence, exploded the entire foundation of petitioners' defense in one sudden and dramatic burst.

Moreover, this was not a case merely of an expression of personal belief in the witness's credibility. Had that been all, petitioners might at least have hoped that the jury would conclude that the United States Attorney was guilty only of bad judgment in believing Baron and that a verdict of acquittal would not be taken by him as a personal affront. The prosecutor, however, went far beyond this. His argument was transparently designed to create in the mind of the jury the impression that a verdict of acquittal would be the equivalent of a charge of perjury against him. In other words, the United States Attorney did not say to the jury merely, "I believe Baron", but rather, "You have no choice but either to believe Baron or to call me a liar!"

To make matters worse, if that were possible, the prosecutor threw into the scales against the defendants the integrity of the highly respected FBI. Since the only FBI witness to appear at the trial testified, without attempt at impeachment, only on the narrow issue of the promises made to Baron (T.T. 307-312), the argument made by the United States Attorney could not have had reference to the credibility of FBI agents as witnesses. Moreover, since the reference was to the FBI generally as an investigative agency, the obvious inference was that that agency, as well as the office of the United States Attorney, was in possession of secret evidence corroborating Baron.

---

otherwise would have been a "weak" case against them. See *United States v. Socony-Vacuum Oil Co.*, 310 U.S. 150, 239 (1940); *Berger v. United States*, 295 U.S. 78, 88-89 (1935).

Finally, it is significant that the argument was made twice, once at the very beginning and once at the very end, thereby assuring the Government that, regardless of the court's rulings, some part of the thought would take root and survive the jury's deliberations. Thus, even had the trial court sustained the objection on the second occasion, the petitioners would have been entitled to a grant of their oral motion for mistrial. (T.T. 521). See *Kitchell v. United States*, 354 F.2d 715 (1st Cir. 1966), where the court said, at 719:

"The government cannot go on, however, making such remarks and having the court strike them out, and then claim they had no effect."

This petition, however, seeks more than a new trial. Petitioners submit that, because of the prosecutor's deliberate conduct in repeating the improper argument, they are entitled to judgments of acquittal as the only appropriate remedy against the harassment of successive prosecutions, see *Downum v. United States*, 372 U.S. 734, 736 (1963), as once suggested by the First Circuit in similar circumstances. *Fleming v. United States*, 332 F.2d 23, 25 (1st Cir. 1964). The deliberateness of the prosecutor is demonstrated not only by his repetition of an argument already once struck by the trial judge, but by his diverting and misleading the trial judge on the occasion of the motion for mistrial and by his later admission in the appellate court that the improper argument was intended as retaliation against the "vicious attacks" of defense counsel. (App. A, 8a).

As to the lower court's holding that it was defense counsel's obligation to suggest that the reporter's notes be read back after the prosecutor twice denied making the offending statements, it should be noted that this solution was equally obvious to the trial judge. He had already characterized the objection as "trivial" and quite obviously did not think the matter important enough to recall the reporter (who had left the courtroom because working in relay with another reporter) and to have him locate the offending passage in his notes. Moreover, the emphatic denials of the prosecutor tended to shake the confidence of defense counsel that they had heard correctly in the first place. A good many of the cases raising the issue of improper argument turn on the failure of defense counsel to interpose timely objection, but now to hold that counsel must presume to guide the court on such obvious matters as the verification of the contents of its own record is to convert the defense of criminal cases into a contest befitting only the most meticulous precisionists. "It would be ignoring the realities of criminal practice to place such a heavy emphasis on the adversary system." See *Harris* v. *United States*, D.C. Cir. 9/17/68, slip op. at 7 (concurring opinion of Bazelon, C. J.).

The importance of these issues in the Federal courts is best demonstrated by the fact that the District of Columbia Circuit recently felt obliged to treat the subject in an extensive dictum "because of the frequent non-observance of the prohibition against expressions of personal opinions on the ultimate issue by counsel." See *Harris* v. *United States, supra* at 4. After further characterizing these frequent breaches of forensic ethics as a "cause for alarm", *id.* at 6, fn. 5, it concluded that, "[s]ince a large number of lawyers — prosecutors and defense attorneys alike — seem to be uninstructed in the rudimentary elements of proper advocacy", it is incumbent on trial judges to supply the necessary instruction, by disciplinary mechanisms if necessary. *Id.* at 6-7. We respectfully submit that, before trial judges can be expected to lay down uniform rules

throughout the Federal system, some initial guidance is
needed from this Court.

C. *The Sufficiency of the Evidence To Establish an
"Attempt"*

An essential element of the substantive crimes charged
in the instant indictment is an "attempt" to commit the
intended murder. The only evidence on the issue was that
defendants pointed out to Baron on two occasions a total
of four or five establishments frequented by the intended
victim, Marfeo. Obviously, the District Court, in denying
motions for judgments of acquittal, disregarded the "well
known" distinction in the criminal law between mere
preparation and attempt. See *Swift & Co. v. United States,*
196 U.S. 375 (1905).

Although the issue was not treated by the Court of
Appeals, because of the imposition of concurrent sentences
on the conspiracy and substantive counts, petitioners intend
to raise the point if certiorari is granted. If there is to
be a new trial on the conspiracy count, we respectfully urge
on the Court the basic unfairness of requiring the defendants simultaneously to defend against substantive charges
of which they are, on the basis of one full trial, wholly
innocent. Cf. *United States v. Bentvena,* 319 F.2d 916,
954-955 (2d Cir. 1963).

Conclusion

For the foregoing reasons, this petition for a writ of
certiorari should be granted.

Respectfully submitted,

Francis J. DiMento
Attorney for Petitioner Patriarca

Ronald J. Chisholm
Attorney for Petitioner Cassesso

Joseph J. Balliro
Attorney for Petitioner Tameleo.

Appendix A

United States Court of Appeals
For the First Circuit

No. 7126.

RAYMOND PATRIARCA,
DEFENDANT, APPELLANT,

v.

UNITED STATES OF AMERICA,
APPELLEE;

No. 7127.

RONALD J. CASSESSO,
DEFENDANT, APPELLANT,

v.

SAME; and

No. 7128.

HENRY TAMELEO,
DEFENDANT, APPELLANT,

v.

SAME.

APPEALS FROM THE UNITED STATES DISTRICT COURT
FOR THE DISTRICT OF MASSACHUSETTS

Before ALDRICH, *Chief Judge,*
McENTEE and COFFIN, *Circuit Judges.*

Francis J. DiMento, with whom *Charles A. Curran* and *DiMento & Sullivan* were on brief, for Raymond Patriarca, appellant.
Ronald J. Chisholm for Ronald J. Cassesso, appellant.
Joseph J. Balliro for Henry Tameleo, appellant.
Edward F. Harrington, Assistant U. S. Attorney, with whom *Paul F. Markham,* United States Attorney, and *Walter T. Barnes,* Special Attorney, Department of Justice, were on brief, for appellee.

October 14, 1968.

COFFIN, *Circuit Judge.* These are appeals from judgments of conviction following jury verdicts on an indictment in three counts. The first count charged all of the appellants with conspiracy, in violation of 18 U.S.C. § 371, to travel and use the telephone in interstate commerce with intent both to commit murder to further an unlawful gambling enterprise, in violation of 18 U.S.C. § 1952(a)(2), and to promote such enterprise, in violation of 18 U.S.C. § 1952(a)(3); and thereafter to attempt to commit such murder and acts of promotion. The chief witness for the prosecution, one Baron, was named as a co-conspirator but not a defendant. Other substantive counts charged appellant Tameleo with using a telephone facility in interstate commerce and appellants Patriarca and Tameleo with causing Baron and appellant Cassesso to travel in interstate commerce pursuant to the same intent, followed by an attempt.

The district court is alleged to have erred in denying a motion for continuance and change of venue because of prejudicial publicity; in refusing to grant a mistrial for prosecutorial expression of belief during the closing argument; and in denying various motions to strike part of the indictment, to grant a severance, to enter judgments of acquittal, and to make a requested instruction.

MOTIONS FOR CONTINUANCE
AND CHANGE OF VENUE

Appellants, in alleging error by the court in refusing their motions for continuance and change of venue filed on February 20, 1968 and at the opening of trial on March 4, 1968, refer in their brief to

"... a long history of publicity, beginning with the widely publicized 'Valachi hearings', so-called, of 1963, which named the defendant Patriarca as 'Boss' of the New England 'Cosa Nostra' or 'Mafia' and the de-

fendant Tameleo as one of his subordinates. It is a
matter of common knowledge that the publicity, surrounding Patriarca, at least, multiplied and persisted
uninterrupted down to May, 1967, when the Government disclosed, in connection with a tax-evasion prosecution in Rhode Island, unconnected with Patriarca,
that his office in Providence had been 'bugged' for
three years and that both he and Tameleo had engaged
in highly compromising conversations with others.''

Subsequently, in May of 1967, newspapers in Boston
published stories that a Mafia ''strongarm'', one Joe (Barboza) Baron, had been ''singing'' to the FBI, referring to
appellant Patriarca as a Cosa Nostra boss. Then on June
20, 1967, the date of the indictment in this case, there were
more newspaper headlines and accounts concerning all appellants and Baron. The newspaper clippings included as
exhibits in the record before us contain no items between
July 10, 1967 and October 27, 1967, when appellant Tameleo was named as having been indicted, after grand jury
testimony by Baron, for a slaying unrelated to these appeals and as being an aide to ''New England Cosa Nostra
boss Raymond Patriarca''.

On October 30, 1967, pursuant to appellants' first motion
for change of venue on July 26, 1967, hearing was had *in
camera*. Counsel for appellant Patriarca, alleging nation-
wide publicity, waived his motion for a change of venue
and requested a continuance of four or five months. The
court stated that the case would not be tried until after the
first of the year and on January 22, 1968 set the date of
trial for February 6.

In the meantime, on January 16, 1968, there had been
several newspaper accounts of the indictment of appellant
Cassesso for conspiracy to incite a fellow prison inmate
to confess falsely to a murder. These, however, were of
small moment compared to the figurative and literal bomb-

shell of January 30, 1968 when Baron's attorney, John E. Fitzgerald, Jr., was almost killed by a bomb wired to the ignition of his automobile. Widespread reporting of and editorializing on the bombing ensued.

On February 2, 1968, appellants moved for a continuance, which was granted until March 4. On February 20 motions for continuance and a change of venue to New York were filed, hearing was had *in camera*, and the motions were denied on February 27, the court observing in a memorandum that the newspaper articles on which the motions were based concerned the Mafia and Cosa Nostra and made no specific reference to defendants; that such articles are constantly appearing in New York as in New England; and that the climate for a fair trial was far more favorable than on October 30, 1967. Similar motions were filed on the day of trial, March 4, based on recent publicity, and were denied for the reasons given on February 27. These two rulings are now before us.

Appellants argue that the prejudice created by the February news accounts, was "the connection of the defendants, in the public's mind, to the bombing incident." The record of newspaper clippings before us, apparently assembled through a clipping service, contains, exclusive of duplications, seventy items from newspapers in Boston and five other major Massachusetts cities covering the period from January 31 to March 4. While not complete and not including any data on television and radio reports, we must take it as reasonably representative. We report the results of our scrutiny in the margin.[1]

---

[1] Articles mentioning the bombing and subsequent investigations were published as follows:

Jan. 31 - Feb. 6 (1 week)	50
Feb. 7 - Feb. 20 (2 weeks)	10
Feb. 21 - Mar. 4 (13 days)	2

In addition, between February 21 and March 4, there were 8 articles reporting only appellants' February 20 request for change of

In none of the newspaper accounts were appellants linked
with the Mafia or Cosa Nostra or with the Fitzgerald bombing. In none were the acts alleged in the indictment reported. In only one article, published one month before
trial, was Baron labelled a Cosa Nostra informer; he was
elsewhere uniformly referred to as an underworld or gangland informer. Even more significant are the facts that
the amount of coverage diminished sharply after the week
following the bombing and that, subsequent to appellants'
filing motions on February 20, the subject matter was almost wholly that of the making and disposition of the motions themselves.

Under these circumstances, we cannot say that the court
abused its discretion. Indeed, the sharp diminution of
decibels after the first week following the Fitzgerald bombing indicates that a month's delay was a realistic estimate.
That a rash of stories centered about moves for further
delay was inevitable; if such could be ground for continuance, cases would never be tried.

We are mindful of the authorities relevant to this issue.
But there is here lacking as of the time of the relevant
motions, the kind of incriminating nexus that was present
in *Rideau* v. *Louisiana,* 373 U.S. 723 (1963) (out of court
confession widely seen); in *United States* v. *Dioguardi,*
147 F. Supp. 421 (S.D. N.Y. 1956) (publicity of recent trial
testimony incriminating defendants); in *Delaney* v. *United*

venue and decision thereon. These made no reference to the bombing.

Only two articles (apart from one report of the court's memorandum of February 27, summarized above) mentioned the Cosa Nostra,
these occurring a month before trial. Two of three articles mentioning Baron as a government witness appeared over a month before
trial as did two references to Fitzgerald being a possible witness.

There was only one reference to appellants Cassesso and Tameleo,
this in connection with another indictment. Of the fourteen references
to appellant Patriarca, one referred to the indictment, five to the
February 2 postponement, and eight to the February 20 motion for
change of venue.

States, 199 F.2d 107 (1st Cir. 1952) (widely publicized Congressional hearings on the "scandal" involving defendant); in *Marshall* v. *United States,* 360 U.S. 310 (1958), and in *Coppedge* v. *United States,* 272 F.2d 504 (D.C. Cir. 1959), *cert. denied,* 368 U.S. 855 (1961) (widespread publicity of excluded or inadmissible information).

Nor do we find a suggestion of the kind of prejudicial statements or records of conviction, arrests, or indictments emanating from a public official, zealous attempts by the media to arouse a community on a particular trial, reports of refusal to submit to certain tests, pejorative characterizations of a defendant, description of evidence against the accused or reports of plea negotiation cited as presenting the "greatest hazards" to a fair trial by the ABA, *Standards Relating to Fair Trial and Free Press.* (Tentative Draft, Dec. 1966), pp. 25-40.[2]

Following the denial of the motions for continuance and change of venue, there was another opportunity for counsel to mitigate any possible effect of pre-trial publicity—on the voir dire. Counsel for one of the appellants requested that the court "ask a question of the jury in connection with this case, in the light of all the publicity." The court replied that it would "put to them a general question and ask them if there is any member of the jury here who feels that he would not be able to give the defendants a fair and impartial trial." Counsel said, "Fine, thank you, your

---

[2] What we have said on the issue of pre-trial publicity also disposes of appellants' motions for severance which were sought on the same basis as the original motions for change of venue, preceding the continuance granted on October 30, 1967, and not thereafter renewed. Absent "a strong showing of prejudice", *Sagansky* v. *United States,* 358 F.2d 195, 199 (1st Cir.), *cert. denied,* 385 U.S. 816 (1966), which we do not find here, it is customary to try conspirators together. *Opper* v. *United States,* 348 U.S. 84, 95 (1959). To the extent that claimed prejudice may arise from association with others, such association would be revealed in any event from the factual situation presented at the trial.

Honor.'' The question was put. No response was forth-
coming. The court stated that it assumed that all were ''in
agreement on this particular question.'' The jurors were
then sworn and thereafter sequestered.

While the court did all that was requested at this junc-
ture, and cannot under the circumstances of this case be
charged with error in not inquiring further, *sua sponte*, we
feel bound to concede that such a single question posed to
the panel en bloc, with an absence of response, achieves
little or nothing by way of identifying, weighing, or re-
moving any prejudice from prior publicity. In cases where
there is, in the opinion of the court, a significant possibility
that jurors have been exposed to potentially prejudicial
material, and on request of counsel, we think that the court
should proceed to examine each prospective juror apart
from other jurors and prospective jurors, with a view to
eliciting the kind and degree of his exposure to the case or
the parties, the effect of such exposure on his present state
of mind, and the extent to which such state of mind is im-
mutable or subject to change from evidence. In this we
are in accord with the suggestions of section 3.4 of ABA,
Standards Relating to Fair Trial and Free Press, (Tentative Draft, Dec. 1966), pp. 130-137.[3]

PROSECUTORIAL SELF-REFERENCE

Appellants seek not only reversal of their convictions
but judgments of acquittal because of the conduct of the
prosecutor in injecting his own belief into his closing argument. They describe the comment as ''outrageous'', in
bad faith, and utterly unprovoked by any defense argu-

---

[3] These pages of the tentative draft were specifically endorsed by
the *Report of the Committee on the Operation of the Jury System on
the "Free Press-Fair Trial" Issue*, p. 39 n. 37. This Report was
formally approved by the Judicial Conference of the United States on
September 19, 1968.

ment. Appellee denies that any comment was made by the prosecutor expressing personal belief in the testimony and that even if such comment were to be so interpreted, it was justified by the "vicious attacks" of appellants' counsel. Finally, appellee argues that the comment could not have been prejudicial. We disagree with all but the last of these positions. We hold that the comment was a prohibited one, to which timely objection was made, that it could not be justified by the argument of appellants' counsel, even though parts of such argument might be interpreted as provocation, but that there was no possibility of its prejudicing the jury under the circumstances of this case. F. R. Crim. P. 52(a).

This conclusion stems from our evaluation of the challenged comment against the background of all the arguments which we now summarize. The gist of the alleged conspiracy was a plan involving the appellants and Baron to kill one Marfeo, the proprietor of a gambling establishment in Providence. This establishment, which continued to operate after once being raided, had caused overt police surveillance in the area to increase to the point where it caused a decline in the patronage of another gambling establishment in which appellant Patriarca allegedly had an interest. Marfeo refused Tameleo's and Patriarca's requests to cease operations and the decision was made to kill him. Baron and appellant Cassesso agreed to do the job, travelled to Providence and viewed places such as restaurants and bars which Marfeo was known to frequent. Further action was postponed since the police had learned of Tameleo's and Patriarca's dispute with Marfeo.

The testimony of Baron was central to the prosecution's case. All of the evidence of the plan, the phone calls, other conversations, travel, and visits to Marfeo's haunts to implement the plan came from his lips. Other witnesses, principally police and federal agents, filled in the background—the raid on Marfeo's establishment, Marfeo's continued operations, accelerated surveillance in the area, a police request to appellant Patriarca to try to persuade Marfeo to close shop, the large scale gambling activities of appellant Tameleo, the identification of places Marfeo frequented.

Baron was a highly vulnerable witness. Not only had he spent almost half of his life in prison, but he had been assured that he would not be indicted for the crime at issue here if he testified before the grand jury. In addition he was told that his cooperation in this matter would be brought to the attention of the prosecution in other pending criminal cases. Money from his unlicensed loan operations continued to be sent to him while in prison. Fears for the safety of his wife and child led to her being allowed to live with him in protective custody. On at least two occasions discussions were had on his behalf with writers relating to a book based on his relevations and movie rights, both promising large returns. Letters which he sent from prison referred to FBI representatives saying to him "If you help us, we will help you"; to the purpose of his transfer to the Barnstable House of Correction as being "to brainwash me"; to having "a few aces" up his sleeve; to his doing something sensational with the result that "30 would go" whether innocent or not. After he began to talk to the FBI about the subject matter of this case, there were some fourteen visits in each of which he would add some new detail either previously overlooked or concealed.

Appellants' three counsel zeroed in on their target. They touched all the bases in vigorous, evocative language. The theme was clearly enunciated in these words of the argument: "I say to you that Mr. Barboza—Mr. Baron—is just a liar. That his story is fiction, and it was made up, coolly calculated, in that very cold blood that he admits he has and for very good reasons." Counsel then colorfully delved into the reasons which he described as "the most tremendous inducements for anybody to lie . . . sex, . . . liberty, and . . . money."

In the course of the ensuing argument for the defense, on the whole proper and evidence-oriented, counsel occasionally made remarks which could be construed as either a personal belief or an attack on the integrity of the prosecution. A failure to introduce evidence alluded to in the prosecution's opening, because of defense counsel's objection, was made the basis for rhetorically asking the prosecution where the promised witnesses were and for remarking to the jury that "that was put in your mind". The word "inducement" was used six times.[4]

The problem with "inducement" is that it does not merely mean "motive". Its primary meaning is "the act or process of inducing", Webster's Dictionary (3d Int. Ed.) p. 1154; it can be easily understood as connoting purpose on the part of the prosecution as well as response on the part of the prospective witness. This possible understanding was reinforced by an appellant's counsel stating, "He is not going to be found guilty of anything"—implying without foundation in the evidence that, with regard to other prosecutions pending against Baron, more than calling the attention of the prosecutor to his cooperation had been promised. A similar observation may be made of counsel's question whether the fact Baron was allowed to live with his wife was "because he is delivering something? Is that the consideration for his being with his wife?" Again the

---

[4] The analysis of the evidence began with the statement "I don't think they [sex, liberty, money] necessarily have to be argued in any particular order, but let's try it this way: inducement." One example referred to the promise of immunity from indictment for the present offense in the words: "I suggest that it is a pretty darned good inducement for some of them to lie and say anything he might think someone wants them to say, because what the heck he doesn't have to worry, he is not going to be indicted."

interpretation of a two-way bargain between the prosecution and Baron for incriminating testimony is not unreasonable. Another oblique remark is a reference to the government's "advantage of everything else they might have going for them here". So also with "Now let me get back to show you the type of job that they are trying to do on my client. . . ." and ". . . I'm going to show you the artfulness in this thing."

One counsel for appellants occasionally also spoke in a way permitting the inference that personal belief was being expressed. For example, "When . . . [Baron] looked at [counsel who was cross-examining] in a cold stare and he said yes, and I have seen a lot of things and I have tried murder cases but it made me wince, and do a little shuddering": ". . . I believe the evidence was that not one of these persons is guilty"; ". . . I think [a verdict of not guilty] is justified by the evidence."

Counsel for the prosecution began by paraphrasing the defense as saying that ". . . Baron's testimony is not fact, it's fiction." He added, "If you accept that, you also accept the fact that that fiction was written, produced and directed by the United States Attorney's office, by the Federal Bureau of Investigation, by the police in Revere and the police in Boston. . . ." Objection was taken and the argument was ordered stricken. The prosecutor then addressed himself to the theme of the defense that Baron had made up the story he told. He sought to verify it by corroboration from other witnesses. In his catalogue of corroboration he cited testimony that Baron knew Tameleo and Cassesso, that Marfeo was running a crap game, that Tameleo was a large scale gambler, that a Providence police captain told Patriarca that he wanted the Marfeo gambling operation closed down, that there was a raid, reconstruction of the premises, renewed operations, increased surveillance or "heat", that Baron's description of the interiors of places of alleged conversations and observations was both detailed and not challenged, that Baron's identification of Marfeo hangouts checked with police identification.

At this point the prosecutor noted the coincidence of police identification of Marfeo hangouts as of a time prior to the alleged conspiracy with that of Baron. He asked if that was fiction. Then he said, "I say that is an insult to your intelligence, and I also say that if Joe Baron is guilty of making it fiction, then I am guilty of making it fiction, and the FBI is guilty of making it fiction and every other witness who testified in this case is guilty of making up fiction." Objection was taken but the court said "That may be argued" and the questioning continued.

A short time later the argument concluded and counsel for appellants moved for a mistrial, citing as a second reason the above quoted argument. The court, referring to its prior ruling at the commencement of the prosecution's argument, asked if the prosecutor had again "put himself in the picture". The prosecutor said, "No, Judge. I said if this is fiction, then every witness who appeared here is fiction." When asked again by the court "You weren't a witness. Did you put yourself in there?" the prosecutor answered, "I asked a few leading questions on occasion, Judge." The court noted that all lawyers commit such an error and denied the motion for mistrial. The case was adjourned overnight and the jury was charged the following day.

The question sharply posed by appellants is whether Rule 15 of the *Canons of Professional Ethics* of the American Bar Association, as applied by us in *Greenberg* v. *United States*, 280 F.2d 472 (1st Cir. 1960), has been violated. *Greenberg* (having to do with a flagrant self-vouching of a prosecutor as a "thirteenth juror") thrusts farther than Rule 15 and some other judicial authorities. Rule 15 pro-

scribes a lawyer from asserting a personal belief in his
client's innocence or the justice of his cause. Such authorities as *Lawn* v. *United States,* 355 U.S. 339, 359-60 n. 15;
Gradsky v. *United States,* 373 F.2d 706, 710 (5th Cir. 1967);
United States v. *Medlin,* 353 F.2d 789, 795 (6th Cir. 1965),
cert. denied, 384 U.S. 973 (1966); *Jones* v. *United States,*
338 F.2d 553, 554 n. 3 (D.C. Cir. 1964); and *United States*
v. *Battiato,* 204 F.2d 717 (7th Cir.), *cert. denied,* 346 U.S.
871 (1953) seem to define the impermissible conduct as any
expression of belief which indicates that the prosecutor is
relying on information other than that which has been presented in court.[5] *Greenberg* proscribes expression of personal belief in the testimony, not only because counsel
would then in effect be a witness not under oath or subject
to cross-examination but because the false issue of credibility of counsel, with government having the advantage,
would be injected.

In *Greenberg* we recognized that at times "special circumstances" may justify a reply but found no such circumstances. Nor do we find such here. We concede that the
prosecutor could interpret parts of the defense argument
as a subtle, veiled attack on the prosecution's motives and
integrity. But we cannot say that counsel for appellants
deliberately indulged in excessive argument. At most their
comments, as we have endeavored to show, were cloaked
in ambiguity. Moreover, if seriously disturbed, counsel for
the government concealed that fact for he raised no objections. At least under these circumstances we do not
consider that a trespass by the defense gives the prosecu-

---

[5] Appellants argue that the prosecutor's reference to the FBI, when
only one agent testified, implied that that agency was in possession of
secret evidence. We think it clear from the context, however, that
the reference was to the corroborating evidence adduced in court which
the prosecutor had just summarized.

tion a hunting license exempt from ethical restraints on advocacy.[6]

Coming to the prosecutor's remarks, we observe first that just as the defense argument was ambiguous, so were these. In context, the prosecutor was pointing to corroborating items of testimony given by police and other witnesses, such as places Marfeo was known to frequent, which matched testimony given by Baron. He was arguing that either such items were true or false. If false, not only one police witness was lying, but all were. And since the instruments of the lies were the prosecutor who asked the questions and the witnesses who answered them, it could arguably be said that on this hypothesis the statement that he was "making fiction" was simply factual and not a statement of belief.

This interpretation, while arguable, is not probable. A more likely interpretation is that this was a back-handed way of laying one's credibility on the line. Prosecuting attorneys and law enforcement officials wear an invisible cloak of credibility by virtue of their position; to make it explicit may too easily tip the scales. Moreover, the same play on the "fiction" metaphor had overcarried earlier, stimulating an objection which was sustained.

Nevertheless, viewing the case as a whole, the arguments, and the charge, we cannot find any possibility of prejudice. First, while the case depended wholly on the credibility of

---

[6] Our approach may differ from some other circuits. If such cases as *Baiocchi v. United States*, 333 F.2d 32, 38 (5th Cir. 1964); *Isaacs v. United States*, 301 F.2d 706, 737 (8th Cir.), *cert. denied*, 371 U.S. 818 (1963); *United States v. Kiame*, 258 F.2d 924, 934 (2d Cir.), *cert. denied*, 358 U.S. 909 (1958); *Ochoa v. United States*, 167 F.2d 341, 344 (9th Cir. 1948); *Malone v. United States*, 94 F.2d 281, 288 (7th Cir.), *cert. denied*, 304 U.S. 562 (1938) stand for the proposition that the mere fact that there has been provocation by the defense justifies retaliatory expression of belief which would otherwise be error, we respectfully disagree. At most, we feel, serious provocation would be weighed as a factor in evaluating possible prejudice.

Baron's testimony, all of the many factors which made it susceptible to impeachment were fully presented and fully argued. The occasional oblique expressions of opinion from both sides against the background of a long trial, much evidence on the issue, and lengthy argument addressed to the evidence could not loom sufficiently large to have influence.[7]

Second, all available timely action was not taken to confront the court with the precise language which had been used. The nature of the objection was not clear to the court at the time, as the subsequent colloquy in the motion for mistrial indicated. The appellants see bad faith in the pro-

---

[7] Our survey of cases involving expression of personal belief has revealed reversals for far grosser improprieties than were exhibited here. *See, e.g., Greenberg, supra; Gradsky, supra,* ("[The government] has every opportunity to check out and judge the credibility and truthfulness of Mr. Zane and Mr. Gilmore in this case, and in that context . . . we offered you this testimony."); *Dunn v. United States,* 307 F.2d 883, 885 (5th Cir. 1962) ("This case is replete with fraud and is one of the most flagrant cases we have ever tried in the Southern District of Georgia.").

We have also noted gross improprieties not resulting in reversals. *See, e.g., Del Cristo v. United States,* 327 F.2d 208, 209 (5th Cir. 1964) ("My final word, ladies and gentlemen, is my sincere belief— and again I must say that defendant's counsel lead you to believe that I don't believe this story, that I am here because I have a job to do—but I believe this man is guilty of the crime charged or I would not be standing here right now prosecuting him. . . ."); *Henderson v. United States,* 218 F.2d 14, 19 (6th Cir.), *cert. denied,* 349 U.S. 920 (1955) ("I am going [to prosecute] . . . if I believe a man guilty. And if I don't believe he is guilty, no one is going to make me . . . prosecute him. . . ."); *United States v. Battiato, supra* at 719 ("If I, in my own mind, thought for one minute that these defendants were not parties to this case I certainly would not have the courage to stand up here and argue before you that they were guilty. It is never our intention to prosecute and try innocent men.")

All of these relied to some extent on the justifying effect of provocation, which we have said we do not recognize as automatically absolving the prosecutor.

We have found no case reversing for a statement of as marginal an impropriety as that here considered, whether or not provocation was present.

secutor's turning off the court's inquiry with a quasi-humorous admission, in answer to a question whether the prosecutor had been a witness and injected himself into his argument, that he had indeed asked a few leading questions. While the prosecutor's answer was clearly not responsive, we do not understand from oral argument that it was devious or calculated to mislead, there having been a superficial response accepted as such at that point. In any event it is clear both that the court did not recall the precise language which the prosecutor had used and that counsel did not feel it important enough to have such language read back. There is an obligation on counsel to make a reasonable effort to see to it that the court has before it the facts on which a requested ruling is predicated. *Cf. Corley v. United States*, 365 F.2d 884, 885 (D.C. Cir. 1966); *Camps v. New York City Transit Authority*, 261 F.2d 320, 323 (2d Cir. 1958). Had this been done, the court, even if it is likely that a mistrial would not have been granted, could have taken pains to devise a proper instruction. For this was not such an egregious comment as to be incurable. As it was, the charge was not given until the following day. The court did include a general instruction that only the evidence must be considered. No special requests were made on this point and no objections taken.

For these reasons we deem this error harmless within the meaning of Fed. R. Crim. P. 52(a).

OTHER ALLEGED ERRORS

Two other asserted errors related to the fact that Baron was named in the indictment as a co-conspirator but not a defendant. The first is that this form of the indictment stemmed from improper prosecutorial influence on the grand jury. The second is that in the course of trial the court went out of its way to say that the government had the privilege not to indict a co-conspirator and in so doing undercut defense efforts to impeach Baron's "inherently suspect testimony".

The first point is based solely on pre-grand jury promises by the prosecutor to Baron that he would not be indicted if he testified. Testimony from an accomplice in a criminal conspiracy is often a *sine qua non* for effective prosecution. *Hoffa* v. *United States,* 385 U.S. 293, 311 (1966). Such testimony will often not be available in the absence of a prosecutor's commitment to grant immunity from prosecution for the criminal acts which are the subject of such testimony. Whether or not a promise of immunity from indictment is technically within the prosecutor's unfettered power to implement, *cf. United States* v. *Cox,* 342 F.2d 167 (5th Cir. 1965), *cert. denied,* 381 U.S. 935, and Fed. R. Crim. P. 48(a), it is highly improbable that a grand jury, on understanding the circumstances resulting in Baron's testimony before it, would indict him. This is entirely proper. Here there is no suggestion of anything more, such as participation by the prosecutor in the deliberations of the grand jury which occurred in *United States* v. *Wells,* 163 Fed. 313 (9th Cir. 1908). Nor have appellants cited any authority requiring that Baron's designation in the indictment as a "coconspirator but not as a defendant" be struck under the circumstances of this case.[8]

Appellants' second contention, that the court erred in twice interjecting the comment in the course of cross-examination about the promise that Baron would not be indicted if he testified to the grand jury, that it was the government's privilege not to indict a co-conspirator as a defendant, is no more substantial. Not only was this a correct statement of the law, *Cox, supra,* but defense counsel made

---

[8] Had the district court granted the request and stricken these words, we do not see how appellants' position would have been improved. The facts surrounding Baron's testimony would necessarily be the battleground of the case.

no objection to the first *sua sponte* comment by the court nor to the same instruction in the final charge. The impeaching effect of the promise of immunity from indictment was not only fully argued at trial but overargued when counsel said ''He is not going to be found guilty of anything''. The court's charge contained standard provisions both as to assessing credibility in general and as to scrutinizing the testimony of an accomplice with great care. Nothing more was requested. We see no error.

Appellants' final argument is that motions for judgments of acquittal on the substantive counts were improperly denied because of a failure of any evidence to establish an ''attempt'' to commit a crime of violence. Both sides agree, however, that the imposition of concurrent sentences on both the conspiracy count and the substantive counts would require decision on this issue only in the event of a new trial.

Affirmed.

19a

Appendix B

United States Court of Appeals
For the First Circuit

No. 7126.

Raymond Patriarca,
DEFENDANT, APPELLANT,

v.

United States of America,
APPELLEE.

JUDGMENT

October 14, 1968

This cause came on to be heard on appeal from the United
States District Court for the District of Massachusetts,
and was argued by counsel.

Upon consideration whereof, It is now here ordered,
adjudged and decreed as follows: The judgment of the
District Court is affirmed.

By the Court:

(s) Roger A. Stinchfield, *Clerk.*

UNITED STATES COURT OF APPEALS
FOR THE FIRST CIRCUIT

No. 7127.

RONALD J. CASSESSO,
DEFENDANT, APPELLANT,

v.

UNITED STATES OF AMERICA,
APPELLEE.

JUDGMENT

October 14, 1968

This cause came on to be heard on appeal from the United States District Court for the District of Massachusetts, and was argued by counsel.

Upon consideration whereof, It is now here ordered, adjudged and decreed as follows: The judgment of the District Court is affirmed.

By the Court:

(s) ROGER A. STINCHFIELD, *Clerk.*

UNITED STATES COURT OF APPEALS
FOR THE FIRST CIRCUIT

No. 7128.

HENRY TAMELEO,
DEFENDANT, APPELLANT,

v.

UNITED STATES OF AMERICA,
APPELLEE.

JUDGMENT

October 14, 1968

This cause came on to be heard on appeal from the United States District Court for the District of Massachusetts, and was argued by counsel.

Upon consideration whereof, It is now here ordered, adjudged and decreed as follows: The judgment of the District Court is affirmed.

By the Court:

(s) ROGER A. STINCHFIELD, *Clerk*.

No. 725

In the Supreme Court of the United States

OCTOBER TERM, 1968

RAYMOND PATRIARCA, RONALD J. CASSESSO, AND
HENRY TAMELEO, PETITIONERS

v.

UNITED STATES OF AMERICA

---

*ON PETITION FOR A WRIT OF CERTIORARI TO THE UNITED
STATES COURT OF APPEALS FOR THE FIRST CIRCUIT*

BRIEF FOR THE UNITED STATES IN OPPOSITION

ERWIN N. GRISWOLD,
Solicitor General,
FRED M. VINSON, Jr.,
Assistant Attorney General,
BEATRICE ROSENBERG,
LAWRENCE P. COHEN,
Attorneys,
Department of Justice,
Washington, D.C. 20530.

INDEX

	Page
Opinion below	1
Jurisdiction	1
Questions presented	1
Statement	2
Argument	14
Conclusion	23

CITATIONS

Cases:

Chapman v. *California,* 386 U.S. 18 15

Greenberg v. *United States,* 280 F. 2d 472 14

Isaacs v. *United States,* 301 F. 2d 706, certiorari denied, 371 U.S. 818 16

Lawn v. *United States,* 355 U.S. 339 16

Myres v. *United States,* 174 F. 2d 329, certiorari denied, 338 U.S. 849 16

United States ex rel. Darcy v. *Handy,* 351 U.S. 454 22

United States v. *Kiamie,* 258 F. 2d 924, certiorari denied, 358 U.S. 909 16

Statute and rule involved:

18 U.S.C. 1952(a) 2

Rule 52 (b) F.R. Crim. P 14

In the Supreme Court of the United States

OCTOBER TERM, 1968

No. 725

RAYMOND PATRIARCA, RONALD J. CASSESSO, AND
HENRY TAMELEO, PETITIONERS

v.

UNITED STATES OF AMERICA

---

*ON PETITION FOR A WRIT OF CERTIORARI TO THE UNITED
STATES COURT OF APPEALS FOR THE FIRST CIRCUIT*

BRIEF FOR THE UNITED STATES IN OPPOSITION

OPINION BELOW

The opinion of the court of appeals (Pet. App. A)
is not yet reported.

JURISDICTION

The judgment of the court of appeals was entered
on October 14, 1968. The petition for a writ of certiorari
was filed on November 12, 1968. The jurisdiction of this
Court is invoked under 28 U.S.C. 1254(1).

QUESTIONS PRESENTED

1. Whether a remark made by the prosecutor in closing argument constituted reversible error.

(1)

2. Whether the trial court properly denied a motion for a change of venue and continuance based on alleged prejudicial publicity.

STATEMENT

After a jury trial, all three petitioners were convicted in the United States District Court for the District of Massachusetts of conspiring to travel and to cause others to travel in interstate commerce with intent to commit murder in order to promote an unlawful enterprise in violation of 18 U.S.C. 1952(a) (2) and (3). In addition, petitioner Patriarca was convicted on a substantive count charging a violation of 18 U.S.C. 1952(a)(2), and petitioner Tameleo on two substantive counts. On March 25, 1968, Patriarca was sentenced to imprisonment for five years and fined $10,000 on the conspiracy count, and to five years on the substantive count, the terms to run concurrently. Tameleo was sentenced to imprisonment for five years and fined $10,000 on the conspiracy count, and to five years on each of the substantive counts, all terms to run concurrently. Cassesso was sentenced to imprisonment for five years and fined $10,000 on the conspiracy count. The court of appeals affirmed the convictions (Pet. App. A).

1. The government's evidence (the sufficiency of which is not challenged as to the conspiracy count) was supplied in most part by the testimony of an unindicted co-conspirator, Joseph Baron. That evidence showed that in March 1965, Tameleo told Baron that he (Tameleo) and Patriarca were having trouble with one Willie Marfeo who was operating a dice game on Federal Hill (Providence, Rhode Island) contrary to

Patriarca's orders. Tameleo told Baron that he had
told Marfeo to close the game because his activities
were drawing "police heat" to the Federal Hill area,
but that Marfeo had not complied (II. 130–132).[1] According to Tameleo, the police had earlier approached
Patriarca and had asked him to use his influence in
closing the game. Patriarca himself attempted to re-
strain Marfeo, but to no avail (II. 132, 133).

On a Monday in late June or early July, 1965,
Tameleo asked Baron and Cassesso to travel from
Boston to Patriarca's office in the Federal Hill area
of Providence, Rhode Island, to help them "solve a
problem" (II. 141–142). Baron telephoned Cassesso
and told him of Tameleo's request (II. 144–147). The
following morning, Cassesso picked up Baron and
drove to Patriarca's office (II. 147–150, 156). Patriarca, Baron and Cassesso engaged in a general
conversation until Tameleo arrived (II. 151). After
Baron said that he had come at Tameleo's request, Patriarca reasserted Tameleo's earlier statement to the
effect that the police had approached him with a request to close down Marfeo's game, that his attempts
to do so had been unsuccessful, and that Marfeo's
continuation of the game and additional "police heat"
had frightened bettors to a point where Patriarca's
own gambling enterprise was suffering (II. 152–153).
After Tameleo mentioned his own unsuccessful attempts to compel Marfeo to close down, Patriarca told
Baron that he wanted Marfeo killed (II. 153–154).

[1] References are to Volumes I–V of the record, all of which
have been filed with the Clerk of this Court.

Although Patriarca said that he would reward them for their efforts, Baron and Cassesso said that they would execute the mission *gratis* (II. 155). At Baron's inquiry, Patriarca said that he wanted Marfeo killed immediately. Patriarca said that he planned to dress Baron and Cassesso as deliverymen in long white coats and scally caps and that they should drive a meat truck to one of Marfeo's "hangouts" where the murder would take place. After assuring Baron and Cassesso that he would have men in the area to take them away, and that he would supply all the equipment needed, Patriarca directed Tameleo to show them the various Marfeo "hangouts" (II. 155–156).

In compliance with Patriarca's direction, Tameleo showed Baron and Cassesso the numerous "hangouts" of Marfeo, which included various bars and restaurants in the Federal Hill area. He also showed them the location where Marfeo was operating the dice game (II. 157–160). Telling Baron and Cassesso that he had to meet some people who would assist in the Marfeo murder, Tameleo then left (II. 160). Baron and Cassesso returned to Boston (II. 160–163).

On the following day, Baron returned to Providence without Cassesso (II. 164). He met Tameleo at a local bar and said that he had returned to get a better picture of the Marfeo "hangouts" (II. 165). At this point, Tameleo told Baron that the police had learned of the argument between him (Tameleo) and Marfeo, and that Patriarca had decided to postpone the murder until the "police heat" had abated (II. 166). At his request, Baron was taken to Patriarca's office. Patriarca stated that he definitely wanted Marfeo killed, but that it should be postponed for a while (II. 166, 167).

Approximately seven to ten days later, Tameleo met with Baron in Revere, Massachusetts. Tameleo said that the "contract" was still on, but that nothing had changed and that the killing should be further postponed (II. 167, 168).

Three days later, Baron and Cassesso returned to Providence. They were told by Patriarca that there were no new developments on the Marfeo "contract", and that they should let the matter "lie for a while" (II. 168). Tameleo again showed them the various Marfeo "hangouts" before they returned to Boston (II. 169–173).

Baron continued his trips to Providence until the fall of 1965 when he was arrested on an unrelated charge (II. 174).

2. Baron's testimony was corroborated in several aspects. Detective-Sergeant William Tocco, Corporal Joseph Broadmeadow, Detective-Trooper Edward Correia, all of the Rhode Island State Police, and Sergeant John Murrary, of the Providence Police Department, testified extensively as to the dice game being operated on Federal Hill by Marfeo (II. 35–60, 69–75, 76–81, 82–104). Detective Edward Walsh of the Boston Police Department testified that, during the pendency of the conspiracy, he had observed Baron and Cassesso together on approximately fifty occasions in the North End of Boston (III. 317). Lieutenant George Hurley of the Revere Police Department testified that, during the same period of time, he observed Tameleo between twenty and thirty

times at the Ebb Tide restaurant in the North End of
Boston, and that on about four of these occasions
Tameleo was with Baron (III. 342, 343). Detective-
Captain John Eddy of the Providence Police Department testified that on March 4, 1965, he had told
Patriarca that Marfeo's dice game had to be stopped
(III. 333–335). Robert Yakubec, an undercover agent
with the Treasury Department, testified extensively
as to the gambling enterprise conducted by Tameleo
in the Federal Hill area. He also testified that
Tameleo's gambling activities subsided substantially
after police activity increased in the area because of
the continuance of Marfeo's dice game (III. 344–398).

3. Petitioners presented no evidence at trial. Their
main defense was an attack upon the credibility of the
government's chief witness, Joseph Baron (see Pet.
11–12). It was shown that Baron had spent approximately half his life in prison for various felonies and
misdemeanors (II. 119–120, 258–263). He was an ad-
mitted "loan shark" (II. 120–121) whose business
continued while he was in prison (II. 228–230).

It was shown that, after his incarceration in the fall
of 1965 on the state firearms charge, Baron was concerned about other, still untried, charges filed against
him (II. 189, 192, 193, 194), and intended to escape
from prison (II. 217). He was first visited by agents
of the F.B.I. on March 8, 1967. On April 13, 1967,
Baron first related the essence of his trial testimony to
the agents (III. 307–311).

It was shown that, when he decided to cooperate,
F.B.I. agents promised that his wife and child would
be granted protection, and that the fact of his cooperation would be brought to the attention of the District

Attorney of Suffolk County and to any presiding judge before whom state indictments would be tried (II. 200; III. 286–287, 310). It was also shown that the United States Attorney had promised that he would not be indicted by federal authorities if he testified before a federal grand jury (II. 184–185; III. 311), and that, although his state sentence for the firearms conviction had not been completely served, he had, since September 1967, been in the protective custody of United States Marshals and permitted to live with his wife in that custody (III. 281).

4. *a.* In closing argument, counsel for Tameleo said (V. 81–82):

> Is Mr. Baron just the ordinary bad guy turned informer? Is he just the stoolpigeon, so to speak that we often hear about in literature and in the movies and on television in connection with criminal trials? No. I say to you, Mr. Foreman and gentlemen, that Mr. Barboza is not a stoolpigeon. He is not an informer in the classic sense we talk about, because a stoolpigeon is someone who has changed his opinion about things that he did and is not telling the truth.
>
> I say to you that Mr. Barboza—Mr. Baron—is just a liar. *That his story is fiction, and that it was made up, cooly calculated, in that very cold blood that he admits that he has and for very good reasons.*
>
> What are the reasons that you should disbelieve Mr. Baron? The remarkable thing—and we will get to those reasons in just a moment, is that with that whole day and part of another day that Mr. Baron was on the stand

as I sat there I didn't get the impression that
there was any reason for his testifying on behalf of the government in this case other than
the three reasons that I am going to suggest
to you now and they are the most powerful
reasons, I think you are going to have to agree,
the most tremendous inducements for anybody
to lie. They are: sex, they are liberty, and they
are money. Those are the three reasons that I
am going to suggest to you that you ought not
to believe Mr. Baron or that any twelve people
who are going to give evidence of a fair shake
must certainly have some reason to doubt what
this man is testifying to about what he wants
you to believe.

I don't think they necessarily have to be
argued in any particular order, but let's try it
this way: *inducement:* Mr. Baron's liberty. Now
you have heard his Honor say that the United
States Attorney has the privilege or right
to say to a man that is going to testify in a
conspiracy charge, "well we're not going to
indict you."

Well, that is all very good to have a privilege
or to have that right, but that certainly does
not make the man any more truthful. As a
matter of fact I suggest that it is a pretty
darned good *inducement* for some of them to lie
*and say anything that he might think someone
wants them to say,* because what the heck he
doesn't have to worry, he is not going to be
indicted. He is not going to be punished.

*　　　*　　　*　　　*　　　*

He is not going to be found guilty of anything. [Emphasis added.]

Enlarging upon this theme, counsel for Tameleo continued:

* * * on March 7, 1967 and on March 8, 1967 in came the Federal Bureau of Investigation agents. Mr. Baron didn't call them in. Do you believe he is telling the story because he is contrite or rehabilitated? He didn't call in the FBI. He didn't call any law enforcement officer in. He didn't say, "I have a story that is on my mind and it's been bothering me and I want to get it off my chest. I want now to be a good citizen." Nothing like that. *The FBI came in to see him on March 8th and what do we find even with regard to March 8th, no story the likes of which you have heard in this courtroom told the agents of the Federal Bureau of Investigation on March 8th, not a word on March 8th* (V. 83). [Emphasis added.]

* * * * *

He is not in solitary isolation any more, Mr. Foreman and gentlemen. He has his wife with him. Now, this man who is serving time in Walpole, and I recall his Honor saying and rightfully so, that every man should have his wife with him. Of course that is true, but are all the other inmates up at Walpole State Prison who are facing yea years in jail with their wives?

What right does this man have to be with his wife, because he is *delivering* something? Is that the *consideration* for his being with his wife? (V. 86). [Emphasis added.]

* * * * *

Before continuing the same line of attack, counsel for Patriarca gave his personal appraisal of Baron, stating (V. 103):

The man is not worthy of belief. When Mr. Balliro asked him did you come down from Providence with the intent to kill Marfeo and he looked at him in a cold stare and he said yes, and I have seen a lot of things and I have tried murder cases but it made me wince, and do a little shuddering.

Resuming the attack on Baron, and the government's case in general, counsel for Patriarca continued:

Now let me get back to show you the type of job that *they* are trying to do on my client Mr. Patriarca. The testimony is that Patriarca is in the coin vending machine office on Atwells Avenue in Providence, Rhode Island. The police came down here and testified they have been on the force for years and he arrives there in the morning and leaves in the afternoon or late afternoon.

He has never been seen in any bars, he has never been seen in any clubs. I think it is a fair inference from the evidence that Patriarca would go to his office during the day, leave at a certain hour and go to his home, as a decent man.

But let's see the reputation *they* are trying to *build up. They* don't bring any body in here to say on such a street in Providence there is a big game going, on Broadway or some other place over near Federal Hill, and that Raymond Patriarca is engaged in it. There are no State Troopers coming in here and testifying that Raymond Patriarca was found in a gambling operation with an apron on and passing out money. There is no such thing as that.

But this is all conjecture, and so forth, and I'm going to show you the *artfulness* of this

11

thing. *They* bring in Captain Eddy. His testimony doesn't mean much, and he is brought in for one purpose. He testified that he had a police officer, Murray or somebody else, go to Raymond's place of business, "Come down to the station".

And then when Raymond gets to the station there is a conversation and Captain Eddy tells him, "We're having a lot of trouble with Marfeo. You've got to do something about it."

Now stop and consider that. Why did *they* pick out Mr. Patriarca? Because he was friendly to Mr. Marfeo, would have influence with him, or because he has some influence on crime—and there is not too much crime in Providence, by the way.

So that *they* go to Raymond and *build him up* as an overlord, or something? That's what I am saying to you (V. 103–105). [Emphasis added.]

*   *   *   *   *

And as Mr. Chisholm well said, do you think this man is going to worry about committing a crime of perjury? This man who is now living with his wife, a fantastic arrangement? Why? Mr. Barbazo is not the type of man that comes in and tells this kind of a story without getting consideration for it and, the evidence was brought out yesterday that he is under the control of the United States Marshals and is having all the bliss of married life. That's quite some punishment, and he is supposed to be doing four to five years (V. 109).

b. Responding to the defense argument that Baron's trial testimony was fiction induced by the government, the United States Attorney began his closing argument by saying (III. 497):

> At the outset, I would like to comment briefly upon defense counsels' arguments.
>
> Basically all of them say that Joseph Baron and Joseph Baron's testimony is not fact, it's fiction. If you accept that, you also accept the fact that that fiction was written, produced and directed by the United States Attorney's office, by the Federal Bureau of Investigation, by the police in Revere and the police in Boston——

On objection of defense counsel, the comment was ordered stricken (III. 497). The United States Attorney then dwelt upon the substantial testimony of six or seven other witnesses, including police officers and federal officers, which corroborated to some extent the testimony of Baron. As he concluded on that theme, the following took place (III. 516–517):

> Now isn't it strange that Tameleo should be taking him (Baron) to these places that I have just mentioned that Sergeant Tocco, Captain Eddy, Sergeant Murray and one or two other officers that I can't name, all identified as Marfeo hangouts? Is that fiction? Did all this testimony from these people who way back in 1965 probably never heard of Joe Baron, all of a sudden just begin to fit together when Joe Baron decides he is going to testify?
>
> I say that it is an insult to your intelligence, and I also say that if Joe Baron is guilty of making it fiction, then I am guilty of making it fiction, and the FBI is guilty of making it a fiction and every other witness who testified in this case is guilty of making up fiction.
>
> Mr. BALLIRO. I object.

The Court. That may be argued.

At the conclusion of all arguments, the following colloquy took place (III. 521-523):

"Mr. Balliro. We move for a mistrial, based upon the grounds——

*   *   *   *   *

"Mr. Balliro. It has to do with the government attorney identifying himself with Mr. Baron to the extent that if this jury believes Mr. Baron and feels he is a liar they also must feel the attorneys for the government and the officers——

"The Court. Strike that out.

"Mr. Balliro. It was left in the last time he argued it again.

"Mr. Markham. I didn't say that.

"The Court. What was that?

"Mr. Balliro. We don't believe that Mr. Markham is a fabricator or anything of that sort. I have known him for a long time and I consider that he is a friend. I think it is prejudicial argument and it sort of puts Mr. Markham in the role of——

"The Court. It is trivial, Joe.

"Mr. Balliro. I think it is an effective argument.

"The Court. I ruled it out at one time when he put himself in the picture. He did it again. Did you do it again?

"Mr. Markham. No, Judge. I said if this is fiction, then every witness who appeared here is fiction.

"The Court. You weren't a witness. Did you put yourself in there?

"Mr. Markham. I asked a few leading questions on occasion, Judge.

"The Court. You all commit that error, but you can't help that. All lawyers do it.

"The motion for mistrial, Mr. Balliro, is denied.

(Adjournment.)"

No request was made for special instructions regarding the alleged prejudicial remark. Prior to closing arguments (V. 70), and again in the general charge (III. 531), the trial court cautioned the jury that statements of counsel were not evidence, and that the case was to be decided on the facts proved at trial. The trial court also instructed that testimony of Baron "should be received with caution and scrutinized with great care" (III. 551).

c. On appeal, the court below held that the prosecutor's argument was proper, except that his reference to his own credibility was improper under its previously announced rule in *Greenberg* v. *United States*, 280 F. 2d 472 (C.A. 1). However, in view of the fact that the remark was ambiguous, that it was in part invited and provoked by defense counsel, and that defense counsel failed to bring the exact nature of the alleged error to the attention of the trial judge and to seek additional cautionary instructions,[2] the court could not find "any possibility of prejudice" (Pet. App. 14a) and the impropriety was, therefore, harmless within the meaning of Rule 52(b), F.R. Crim. P.

ARGUMENT

1. The court below properly held that, in context, the remarks of the prosecutor did not constitute

---

[2] The charge was not given until the following day.

reversible error. It is evident that the prosecutor did not intend to bring himself personally into the picture, and was not certain that he had done so on the occasion of the motion for a mistrial. To the extent that he did refer to his own credibility, the court of appeals correctly held that this ambiguous, passing reference did not, in context, cause "any possibility of prejudice" (Pet. App. 14a). That standard of review amply complies with an appellate court's responsibility in deciding that error was harmless. *Chapman* v. *California*, 386 U.S. 18.

In their principal thrust, the prosecutor's challenged remarks were a defense of the integrity of all the government witnesses against the unsupported charges of defense counsel. The remarks not stricken were made after the prosecutor had summarized the corroborating evidence given by witnesses who were government employees. Their purpose was to refute the aspersions cast by defense counsel on the character of the government as a whole.

On the facts of this case, the court below correctly held that these remarks of the prosecutor were justified. As set forth above, defense counsel went beyond the limits necessary for a proper attack upon the credibility of Baron and, in doing so, put the integrity of the government in issue. Not content to rest upon Baron's unsavory character and prior transgressions, counsel for Tamelco emphasized that his "fiction" was "induced" by certain promises made, assured, and carried out, by government officials, and that these "inducements" were very good instruments to make Baron "lie and say anything that he might think someone wants them to say, because what the heck he doesn't have to worry, he is not going to be indicted. He is not going to be punished. * * * He is not going to be found guilty of anything" (V. 82). Whether intended or not, the import of the argument was that Baron's testimony was a "fiction" authored, not only by Baron, but by all the officials involved, including the witnesses and even the United States Attorney. Counsel for Patriarca continued this line of argument, even more explicitly. Alluding to what he alleged to be a calculated scheme to convict his client on no evidence, counsel cautioned the jury, "Now let me get back to show you the type of job *they* are trying to do on my client, Mr. Patriarca" (V. 103). (Emphasis added.) He asked the jury to "* * * see the reputation *they* are trying to *build up.*" (V. 104) (emphasis added), and to see "* * * the *artfulness* of this thing [the government's case]" (V. 104). He asked "Why did *they* pick out Mr. Patriarca?" (V. 104) (emphasis added), and finally argued that "* * * *they* go to Raymond and *build him up* as an overlord, or something" (V. 104–105). (Emphasis added.)

Petitioners are in no position to complain about the remarks which were invited and provoked by their own improper arguments. See *Lawn* v. *United States,* 355 U.S. 339, 359–360, n. 15; *Isaacs* v. *United States,* 301 F. 2d 706, 738 (C.A. 8), certiorari denied, 371 U.S. 818; *United States* v. *Kiamie,* 258 F. 2d 924, 934 (C.A. 2), certiorari denied, 358 U.S. 909; *Myres* v. *United States,* 174 F. 2d 329, 339 (C.A. 8), certiorari denied, 338 U.S. 849.

Moreover, the trial judge specifically instructed that comments of counsel were not evidence, and that Baron's testimony was to be received with caution and to be scrutinized with great care, all of which militated against possible prejudice.

2. On July 26, 1967, petitioners moved for a change of venue on the grounds of alleged prejudicial publicity (I. 4–5). Up to the time of argument on the motion on October 30, 1967, newspaper articles had identified Patriarca as head of the Cosa Nostra in New England, had referred to Baron's cooperation with the F.B.I., and had reported the present indictment and the fact that Marfeo had later been murdered.[3]

---

[3] On May 21, 1967, and again on May 23, two newspaper articles referred to Patriarca as the head of the Cosa Nostra in New England (IV. 1–2, 3). On May 25, and again on May 26, two newspaper articles reported that Baron had begun to cooperate with the F.B.I. (IV. 4, 5).

On June 20 and 21, various newspapers reported that petitioners had been indicted for the crimes proved herein. These articles reported the nature of the indictment, and the fact that Marfeo subsequently had been murdered. They also mentioned that Baron was a "key" to the case, and included a biography of Baron (IV. 7–10, 11, 12–14). On June 22, one newspaper reported that an arraignment would follow, that the United States Attorney hailed the indictment as a major step against organized crime, and that the indictment had been obtained as a result of the "singing" of Baron (IV. 15). Another reported Baron's biography (I. 16). On June 26, an article stated that Patriarca and Cassesso had entered pleas of not guilty at the arraignment. This article also mentioned that Patriarca reputedly was a leader of the Cosa Nostra (I. 17–18).

On July 20, 1967, one article reported that Baron was still cooperating with the F.B.I., and editorially extolled the value of an informer in the fight against organized crime (IV. 19).

On October 27, 1967, an article reported that Tameleo had been indicted by the State of Massachusetts for conspiring to murder one Edward "Teddy" Deegan (IV. 20).

On October 30, all petitioners substituted a motion for a continuance for the motion for change of venue (I. 6, 7, 8; V. 2–4). At that time, counsel for Patriarca recognized that the existence of the Cosa Nostra, and the fact that Patriarca was reputedly the head of the New England activities, were facts well known throughout the country. He indicated that Patriarca preferred to be tried in Massachusetts (V. 2–4). The case was subsequently set for February 6, 1968 (V. 58).

On January 30, 1968, a bombing attempt was made on the life of John E. Fitzgerald, Jr., an attorney representing Joseph Baron. On January 31, various newspapers in Boston and the nearby New England area reported the facts surrounding the bombing attempt. The newspapers speculated that the bombing was of a "gangland" nature, and reported that Fitzgerald represented Baron who had earlier testified in a state case involving a gangland murder (IV. 26–28, 29–31, 32–34, 35). One newspaper reported that Baron was scheduled to testify in a federal case (IV. 28), but neither the nature of the case nor the defendants were mentioned. On February 1 and 2, approximately seventeen articles contained further reports concerning the Fitzgerald bombing, and editorially demanded legislative and executive action. Although several mentioned that Baron had testified in the state case, none of the present petitioners was mentioned by name (IV. 36–58). In one newspaper it was reported that the United States Attorney would neither confirm nor deny speculation that Fitzgerald "was listed as a prospective witness in a racketeering prosecution scheduled to begin shortly in a Federal Court here" (IV. 45). Neither the nature of the case nor the names of the defendants were mentioned in the article.

On February 2, 1968, petitioners moved for a further continuance because of publicity concerning the bombing attempt against Fitzgerald. On the basis of these motions, trial was set for March 4 (I. 14).

On February 20, 1968, petitioners again moved for a change of venue and a continuance on the ground of alleged prejudicial publicity.[4] Those motions, as

---

[4] On February 3, one article mentioned that a local district attorney had been threatened in typical gangland fashion (IV. 59), and others demanded immediate legislative action (IV. 60, 64–65). Four articles also reported that Judge Ford had granted petitioners a continuance without comment. In these latter reports, it was mentioned that petitioners' moving affidavits in support of the motions for a continuance had cited the Fitzgerald bombing publicity as prejudicial to their case (IV. 59, 61, 62–63).

The publicity of February 4 and 5 focused upon medical and investigative progress reports on the Fitzgerald bombing, and organized crime in general (IV. 66–67, 73, 74–75, 76–77, 78, 79–80, 81, 82). One newspaper included a biography of Fitzgerald, and mentioned that petitioners had based their motion for a continuance on the publicity surrounding the attempt on his life since he was listed as a prospective witness in their case. The article went on to say, however, that the United States Attorney had serious doubts as to the importance of Fitzgerald as a witness (IV. 68–72).

Progress reports—medical and investigative—continued on February 6. Various other articles also mentioned that a reporter had received a gangland threat, that Cassesso and Tameleo had been arraigned in the Deegan murder case, and that a local criminal case—handled by Fitzgerald's law partner—had been continued (IV. 83–88, 90–91).

From February 7 through February 19, miscellaneous reports on the Fitzgerald bombing, and public reaction thereto, continued (IV. 89, 92–100). One report mentioned that a reporter

well as similar motions made on the first day of trial, were denied (I. 41–42; II. 214).

In a written memorandum denying the motions, Judge Ford said, *inter alia* (I. 41):

> The motions are based generally on articles appearing in press media concerning the Mafia and Cosa Nostra. They are not based on articles that have specific reference to any of the defendants.
>
> The motions request a transfer of the case to the Southern District of New York where, there and elsewhere in the United States, like articles concerning Cosa Nostra and the Mafia are constantly appearing as they are in the New England States.
>
> This case must be tried at some point and to delay this case or transfer it to a jurisdiction where such articles will cease to be published would result, in the judgment of this Court, that the case would never come to trial.

---

had been threatened (IV. 92), and another—directed at the organized crime situation in Massachusetts—indicated that the United States Attorney had obtained a federal indictment against Patriarca (IV. 93).

On February 21, one article reported that petitioner had moved for a change of venue (IV. 101); on February 27, that the motions had been taken under advisement (IV. 102); and on February 28, that the motions had been denied (IV. 103, 104).

On March 1, one newspaper reported that the State Commissioner of Correction had sought legislative approval of a bill which would permit the transfer of state prisoners to federal institutions so as to afford protections to such prisoners as "Joseph Baron" (IV. 105). Another reported that the State Commissioner did not know the present whereabouts of Baron who was scheduled to be a witness at petitioner's trial (IV. 105).

On March 4, 1968, one newspaper heralded the beginning of petitioners' "much delayed" trial (IV. 106).

Finally the climate with respect to the defendants' securing a fair and impartial trial is not adverse and is far more favorable than on October 30, 1967 when all defendants waived their motions for a change of venue.

* * * * * ·

In the circumstances, the trial court properly denied the latter two motions for a change of venue and a continuance. Although petitioners have accumulated numerous newspaper items dating back to May 1967 which they claim to have been prejudicial, their argument in this Court is directed exclusively to the publicity surrounding the Fitzgerald bombing (Pet. 15–17). Contrary to petitioner's suggestion, however, that publicity was not prejudicial to the trial of their case. As emphasized by the court below, and as amply demonstrated by the exhibits introduced prior to trial, not one item of that publicity up to and including February 2, 1968—when petitioners moved for a continuance—suggested, or even hinted, that petitioners were connected with the bombing. Indeed, the inference attributable to that publicity was that certain local "gangland" defendants, against whom Baron had testified in a state criminal case, had been responsible for the attempt on Fitzgerald's life (see, *e.g.,* IV. 26–28, 29–31, 35, 37, 44, 48). The one item which reported that Baron was scheduled to testify in a federal case (IV. 28), and the other which speculated that Fitzgerald "was listed as a prospective witness in a racketeering prosecution" scheduled for the federal district court (IV. 45), were, for any but the most sophisticated reader, innocuous, since neither the nature of the case (beyond its terse description as a "racketeering prosecution"), nor the names of the defendants therein, were identified. Nevertheless, the trial judge, in an abundance of caution, granted a continuance for one month (V. 65–68).

Thereafter—aside from the speculative publicity of February 3 and 4 engendered by petitioners' motion papers filed on February 2, 1968 (IV. 59, 61, 62–63, 68–72)—no publicity connected, or attempted to connect, petitioners with the Fitzgerald bombing. And as noted by the trial court and court below, publicity with respect to the bombing incident had completely abated by the time of trial.[5] In these circumstances, petitioners have failed to establish "as a demonstrable reality" that unfavorable publicity "create[d] such an atmosphere that it infected the jurors and deprived petitioner[s] of a fair trial on the evidence * * *" *United States ex rel. Darcy* v. *Handy,* 351 U.S. 454, 462, 463.[6]

---

[5] The jury was sequestered during the trial (Pet. App. 7a).

[6] Although petitioners briefly allude (Pet. 6) to publicity concerning electronic overhearings, there is no claim here concerning the overhearings themselves. Prior to trial, the Department of Justice turned over to the clerk of the district court all logs of electronic overhearings which related to petitioners. These logs, in turn, were inspected by counsel who represented petitioners at trial. No motions were made in the district court with regard to the logs.

CONCLUSION

For the reasons stated, it is respectfully submitted that the petition for a writ of certiorari should be denied.

ERWIN N. GRISWOLD,
Solicitor General.
FRED M. VINSON, Jr.,
Assistant Attorney General.
BEATRICE ROSENBERG,
LAWRENCE P. COHEN,
Attorneys.

DECEMBER 1968.

In the
Supreme Court of the United States

OCTOBER TERM, 1968

No. 725

RAYMOND PATRIARCA, RONALD J. CASSESSO
and HENRY TAMELEO,

PETITIONERS,

v.

UNITED STATES OF AMERICA,

RESPONDENT.

PETITION FOR REHEARING OF ORDER DENYING PETITION FOR A WRIT OF CERTIORARI TO THE UNITED STATES COURT OF APPEALS FOR THE FIRST CIRCUIT

FRANCIS J. DIMENTO
100 State Street
Boston, Massachusetts 02109
Tel: (617) 523-5253
Attorney for Petitioner Patriarca

RONALD J. CHISHOLM
261 Tremont Street
Boston, Massachusetts 02116
Tel: (617) 426-8688
Attorney for Petitioner Cassesso

JOSEPH J. BALLIRO
44 School Street
Boston, Massachusetts 02108
Tel: (617) 227-5822
Attorney for Petitioner Tameleo

Blanchard Press, Inc., Boston, Mass. — Law Printers

In the
Supreme Court of the United States

No. 725

RAYMOND PATRIARCA, RONALD J. CASSESSO and HENRY TAMELEO,
PETITIONERS,

v.

UNITED STATES OF AMERICA,
RESPONDENT.

PETITION FOR REHEARING OF ORDER DENYING PETITION FOR A WRIT OF CERTIORARI TO THE UNITED STATES COURT OF APPEALS FOR THE FIRST CIRCUIT

Petitioners pray that this Court grant rehearing of its order of January 13, 1969, denying their petition for a writ of certiorari and that a writ of certiorari issue to review the judgment of the Court of Appeals for the First Circuit in the above-entitled case as prayed for in their petition filed herein on November 12, 1968.

Further Questions Presented

1. Did the Government's guarantee of immunity from prosecution and the grant of other favors to an accomplice,

who was the sole witness to the *corpus delicti*, violate the
standards of procedural fairness applicable to a so-called
one-witness case so as to require the corrective exercise
of this Court's supervisory powers?

2. Did the trial court's instructions to the jury that it
is the Government's privilege not to indict a co-conspirator,
given during the course of cross-examination by defense
counsel, similarly violate the applicable standards of pro
cedural fairness?

Reasons for Granting Rehearing and
Issuing the Writ

Since the original petition was filed in this case the
Court of Appeals for the Fourth Circuit has had occasion
to re-examine the so-called, common law "one witness
rule" to the effect that the testimony of a single witness
is generally sufficient to warrant conviction. In re affirm
ing the rule, that court added the qualification that a trial
judge "has the power to refuse to permit a criminal case
to go to the jury even though the single eyewitness testi
fies in positive terms . . ." *United States* v. *Levi*, 4th Cir.,
Dec. 19, 1968, *slip op.* at 6. Although the court wrote in
the context of the possibly mistaken identification testimony
of a single eyewitness, it also recognized the applicability
of its holding to possible instances of "false swearing."
Id. at 4.

Thus, given the one-witness rule as laid down in *Hoffa*
v. *United States*, 385 U.S. 293 (1966), the Fourth Circuit
has now raised the question whether, and to what extent,
the federal appellate courts ought to exercise their supervisory powers to insure fairness in such cases. In the
original petition for grant of a writ of certiorari, petitioners contended that the limits of fairness had been over-
stepped where the single-witness case against them had

been tried in an atmosphere of prejudicial publicity and where the prosecutor had deliberately thrown onto the scales his own integrity and that of non-witness agents of the FBI. Now, in the new light of the *Levi* case, suggesting that a higher standard of procedural fairness may be applicable to the single-witness case, petitioners wish to focus more sharply on the supervisory powers of the appellate courts in such cases and to offer further considerations in evaluating their claim that their convictions resulted from a combination of inequities which converted an otherwise close issue of credibility into easy victory for the prosecution.

The witness Baron testified on cross-examination that he had been told he would not be indicted if he testified before the grand jury (T.T. 185). Moreover, Agent Dennis Condon of the FBI testified at the trial that the United States Attorney, himself, had told Baron, in Condon's presence, that he would not be indicted (T.T. 311-312). On each occasion that this testimony was elicited, the trial court, *sua sponte*, instructed the jury that

> "it is the privilege of a United States Attorney not to indict a co-conspirator as a defendant" (T.T. 312, 185),

and again in the course of its formal charge to the jury, stated:

> "It is not fatal to the government's case, in a conspiracy case, if it chooses, which is its right, to name certain persons as co-conspirators and not name them as defendants." (T.T. 545).

As demonstrated in the original petition, the principal issue at the trial was the credibility of Baron, the Gov-

ernment's sole witness to the *corpus delicti*. Indeed, Mr.
Baron's testimony was so highly motivated as to raise
serious doubt whether any conviction resting exclusively
on such testimony should stand. The situation was no less
extreme than that in *Hoffa v. United States*, 385 U.S. 293
(1966), where Chief Justice Warren, in a dissenting opinion, was moved to say of the Government's chief witness,
at 317-318:

> "Here, Edward Partin, a jailbird languishing in a
> Lousiana jail under indictments for such state and
> federal crimes as embezzlement, kidnapping, and man-
> slaughter (and soon to be charged with perjury and
> assault), contacted federal authorities and told them
> he was willing to become, and would be useful as, an
> informer against Hoffa who was then about to be
> tried in the Test Fleet case. A motive for his doing
> this is immediately apparent—namely, his strong de-
> sire to work his way out of jail and out of his various
> legal entanglements with the State and Federal Gov-
> ernments."

And, further, at 320:

> "This type of informer and the uses to which he
> was put in this case evidence a serious potential for
> undermining the integrity of the truth-finding process
> in the federal courts. Given the incentives and back-
> ground of Partin, no conviction should be allowed to
> stand when based heavily on his testimony . . . For
> the affront to the quality and fairness of federal law
> enforcement which this case presents is sufficient to
> require an exercise of our supervisory powers."

It is true that federal courts have consistently held the

uncorroborated testimony of accomplices, or testimony made after promises and inducements, to be competent and admissible as evidence. See, *e.g., United States* v. *Vida,* 370 F.2d 759, 767-768 (6th Cir. 1966) (and cases cited); *Diaz-Rosendo* v. *United States,* 357 F.2d 124, 130 (9th Cir. 1966). But misgiving arising even in the ordinary case from the danger of untrustworthinesss of such information is reflected in the concomitant rule that such testimony must be considered with great care and caution. As recently as last May, in *Bruton* v. *United States,* 391 U.S. 123 (1968), this Court said with respect to the incriminations of an accomplice, at 136:

> "their credibility is inevitably suspect, a fact recognized when accomplices do take the stand and the jury is instructed to weigh their testimony carefully given the recognized motivation to shift blame onto others."

The judicial reluctance to lay down a protective rule excluding such highly motivated testimony has meant that the only protection lies with the jury and whatever hesitancy it may have in believing such suspect testimony.

Accordingly, defendants are entitled to wide latitude in this respect with the jury. See *On Lee* v. *United States,* 343 U.S. 747 (1952), where the Court said at 757:

> "The use of informers, accessories, accomplices, false friends, or any of the other betrayals which are 'dirty business' may raise serious questions of credibility. To the extent that they do, a defendant s entitled to broad latitude to probe credibility by cross-examination and to have the issues submitted to the jury with careful instructions."

Minimally defendants are entitled to preserve their position with the jury on this important point of credibility and not have it undercut by remarks of the court which have the tendency to support what is inherently suspect testimony. Whether or not the instructions were a correct statement of the law,[1] their timing was particularly injurious. By stating, just at the time when defense counsel was making the point as to the inducements held out to Baron to testify, and again in its charge, that the Government had the right to make such promises, the trial judge distracted the jury from the issue of Baron's credibility and obviated any hesitancy it otherwise would have had to believe Baron.

Concededly the trial court did include one sentence in its charge, and one sentence only, expressing the rule of caution. (T.T. 551). However, by consistently implying that such promises or inducements as had been made to Baron were perfectly proper and usual, the court effectively negatived the reason why the jury should be cautious. If juries are to be permitted to believe such testimony, because courts are unwilling to declare it incompetent as matter of law despite its inherent untrustworthiness, it is fundamentally unfair for a court to step in and buttress the Government's case by indicating that what was done by way of inducement was proper.

Moreover, by guaranteeing its chief witness immunity and bestowing other favors on him in exchange for his testimony, the Government seized an advantage wholly unavailable to the defendants, who had no similar means of wringing testimony from witnesses fearful of self-incrimination.

In dismissing these arguments, the Court of Appeals re-

___

[1] Petitioners suggest that it is the "privilege" of the *Grand Jury,* not of the Government, to indict or not to indict.

lied on the fact that "defense counsel made no objection to the first *sua sponte* comment by the court nor to the same instruction in the final charge." See original Petition, pp. 17a-18a. The reason, of course, that no objection was made on the first occasion was that defense counsel did not wish to compound the damage by inviting further comment from the trial judge. On the second occasion, counsel realized that, short of a corrective instruction, the damage was now irreparable and, accordingly, entered their objection. Having once preserved their rights on the record, counsel saw nothing further to be gained by a futile objection to the same instruction during the course of the formal charge to the jury.

Where, as here, the government's case "rested entirely upon the uncorroborated testimony . . . of an accomplice and co-conspirator who had the strongest possible reasons to become a Goverment witness," it is incumbent upon this Court to "scrutinize any claimed error with extreme care since there is grave possibility of prejudice to the defendants in a case such as this by error which might in other circumstances be deemed relatively minor." *United States* v. *Persico*, 305 F.2d 534, 536 (2d Cir. 1962).

In summary, petitioners concede that the testimony of a single witness, who is also an accomplice, may be sufficient to sustain a conviction. On the other hand, if the rule of the Fourth Circuit as laid down in *Levi* is correct, and assuming the continued vitality of the language in *Bruton*, then petitioners contend that they are entitled to the highest procedural protection of which our trial courts are capable. As demonstrated in their original Petition, the atmosphere in which the trial was held and the conduct of the prosecutor did nothing to contribute to the attainment of these high standards. As argued here, the guarantee of immunity and the grant of other favors, which defense counsel could not hope to match in obtaining witnesses favorable to the defendant, and the intrusive instructions of the trial judge at critical points of cross-examination by defense counsel served further to enlarge the gap by which petitioners' trial fell short of the high standards of fairness applicable to the single-witness case.

This petition, therefore, presents a full range of issues typical of the case which rests entirely on the testimony of a single informer, including the means employed by the prosecutor to obtain the cooperation of the witness, the atmosphere of the trial, the conduct of the prosecutor and defense counsel, and the responsibilities of the trial court in instructing the jury and insuring procedural fairness. These issues, it is submitted, afford the Court a rare opportunity to enunciate and clarify the special rules of procedural fair play applicable to the single-witness case.

Conclusion

For the reasons set forth above and in the petition for a writ of certiorari, it is respectfully urged that rehearing be granted and that, upon such rehearing, a writ of certiorari issue to the Court of Appeals for the First Circuit.

Respectfully submitted,

FRANCIS J. DiMENTO
Attorney for Petitioner Patriarca

RONALD J. CHISHOLM
Attorney for Petitioner Cassesso

JOSEPH J. BALLIRO
Attorney for Petitioner Tameleo

Certificate of Counsel

We hereby certify that the foregoing petition for rehearing is presented in good faith and not for delay and is restricted to grounds specified in Rule 58 of the rules of this Court.

FRANCIS J. DIMENTO
Attorney for Petitioner Patriarca

RONALD J. CHISHOLM
Attorney for Petitioner Cassesso

JOSEPH J. BALLIRO
Attorney for Petitioner Tameleo

FILED

FEB 13 1969

JOHN F. DAVIS, CLERK

IN THE

SUPREME COURT OF THE UNITED STATES

OCTOBER TERM, 1968

NO. 726

FRANK SUTTON, on behalf of
himself and others similarly
situated,

                    Appellant,
        vs.

TOM ADAMS, as Secretary of State
of the State of Florida and
EARL FAIRCLOTH, as Attorney
General of the State of Florida,

                    Appellees.

PETITION FOR REHEARING
OF DISMISSAL OF APPEAL

MILTON E. GRUSMARK and
NATALIE BASKIN
Attorneys for Appellant
1674 Meridian Avenue
Miami Beach, Florida 33139

INDEX

                                                    Page

PETITION

        I   1

        II   2

        III   3

        IV   6

CONCLUSION   7

CERTIFICATE OF MAILING   8

DECISION, SUPREME COURT OF THE
UNITED STATES   APPENDIX A

   CERTIFICATE OF GOOD FAITH   APPENDIX B

AUTHORITIES

Page

Epperson v. Arkansas, ___U.S.___,
___S.Ct.___, 21 L.Ed.2d 228 (1968)   5, 6,

Mills v. Alabama, 384 U.S. 214, 16
L.Ed.2d 484, 86 S.Ct. 1434 (1966)   2, 4

FLORIDA STATUTES

    F.S. 99.161(1)(b)   1, 3
    F.S. 99.161(2)(a)(b)   3, 4
    F.S. 104.27   3

On January 20, 1969, this Court dismissed
the appeal for want of a substantial federal
question. A copy of the decision is appended.

Appellant urges this Court to grant rehearing because substantial federal questions
are raised by the denial of rights under the
Constitution of the United States.

Constitutional rights and consequent
federal questions are presented in this appeal
concerning freedom of speech, voting in
national elections, and due process of law.

I

The right to vote has been abridged by
Florida Statute 99.161(1)(b). The right to
vote is not limited to the mere casting of
a ballot. Voters participate in national
elections by electing as state officers quali-
fied electors. There is no other manner by
which a voter can participate in a presidential
election. If the right to vote for electors
is curtailed, the right to vote in national
elections is equally abridged.

Federal rights are involved since federal
elections are involved. The Florida resident
participates in national elections through
support of a state official, an elector, who
then votes for president and vice-president
of the United States.

II

The right to freedom of speech is denied
by the challenged statute. The importance of
this right to freedom of speech, particularly
when that right is involved in an election,
was affirmed by this court, Mills v. Alabama,
384 U.S. 214, 16 L.Ed.2d 484, 86 S.Ct. 1434
(1966). In that case the Court considered
the right to publish an editorial on an
election day as a violation of the Alabama
Corrupt Practices Act. The Court stated:

> "Whatever differences may exist
> about interpretations of the
> First Amendment, there is prac-
> tically universal agreement that
> a major purpose of that Amendment
> was to protect the free discussion
> of governmental affairs. This of
> course includes discussions of
> candidates, structures and forms
> of government, the manner in
> which government is operated or
> should be operated, and al' such
> matters relating to political
> processes."

In their concurring opinion Mr. Justice
Douglas and Mr. Justice Brennan stated that
the rights of free speech and free press
in a basic form were concerned, namely the
right to express views on matters before
the electorate.

The same needs and the same rights are concerned in the case at bar. The broad term "contribution" and its prohibition to a liquor licensee, severely restrict society as well as the licensee. The literal right to freedom of speech is violated because the licensee is prohibited not only from contributing in the form of speeches made by himself, but from hiring persons who may speak in whatever appropriate form is available as well.

III

A substantial federal question is raised by the challenge to Florida Statute 99.161 (1)(b) on the grounds that it is unconstitutionally vague, constituting a deprivation of due process of law.

Because the nature of prohibited contributions is undefined by the statute, there is no guideline for a liquor licensee to follow. Nevertheless, criminal sanctions are applied for violations: Florida Statute 104.27.

When the statute is read in pari materia with other portions of the statutes concerned, as suggested by Appellees, it becomes clear that the legislature omitted the very definitions found in Section 99.161(2)(a)(b). The absence of clarifying definitions renders the statute vague.

The Court overlooked and failed to consider the fact that the argument that the statutes

3.

should be read in pari materia supports
Appellant's position and not Appellees' posi
tion.

It is contended that the specific inclusi
of contributions that are prohibited in Sect
99.161(2)(a) and (b) such as money, material.
supplies or loans are applicable to liquor
licensees.

On the contrary, the challenged statute nc
provides for a distinction between the gener:
public and the prohibitions contained in 99.1
(2)(a) and (b) and the prohibitions applicabl
to liquor licensees. In the statute under
attack, a liquor licensee is not proscribed
as is the general public merely from giving
money, materials, loans, etc., he is prohibit
from making a contribution "of any nature".
The difference is the difference enacted by
the legislature. Either the language "of any
nature" is so meaningless as to be vague and
unconstitutional, or it prohibits political
support in any way. If it does, it is contra:
to the philosophy stated in Mills, supra, and
invades the constitutional rights of a liquor
licensee.

In his opinion in the case at bar, Supreme
Court of Florida Justice Thornal, concurring
in part and dissenting in part, stated:

> "I would strike from the statute
> the underscored proviso quoted
> in the opinion by Justice Drew.

4.

The legislature might have
intended what the opinion
assumes but it certainly did
not so state. I fear that the
opinion merely supplies a
judicial assumption of legislative intent, contrary to the
expressed language of the enact-
ment. The proviso, I think,
is unconstitutional. I would
strike it and permit the re-
mainder of the statute to stand.
I concur in part and dissent in
part."

In Epperson v. Arkansas, ___U.S.___,
___S.Ct.___, 21 L.Ed.2d 228 (1968), this
court was concerned with a vague statute.
In his concurring opinion Mr. Justice Black
stated:

"It is an established rule that
a statute which leaves an ordinary
man so doubtful about its meaning
that he cannot know when he has
violated it denies him the first
essential of due process. See,
e.g., Connally v. General Construc-
tion Co., 269 U.S. 385, 391, 70
L.Ed. 322, 328, 46 S.Ct. 126
(1926)."

A further denial of due process of law
arises from the absence of a reasonable classi-
fication for excluding liquor licensees from

exceptions to the statute available to member
of country clubs, social and fraternal associ
tions and cultural organizations. Refusal tc
permit members of corporations holding liquor
licenses to make contributions permitted by
members of corporations in the privileged
category of corporations holding liquor licen
is purely arbitrary.

The Supreme Court of Florida stated in its
opinion that the statute was not meant to be
interpreted literally, out of context. Howev
in the absence of a literal interpretation,
and the absence of guidelines for any other
interpretation, it is impossible for due
process of law to be accorded.

IV

Under Epperson, supra, this Court will
review constitutional questions concerning
the propriety of a statute although those
questions were not specifically ruled on by
the state court.

In Epperson, supra, this Court decided
issues brought before it on appeal, although
the state court did not address itself to
certain constitutional considerations. This
court held its duty to be to decide the issue
presented to it.

In the present case, the statute was de-
clared unconstitutional by the trial court on
one ground, so that other grounds were not

6.

required to be considered. Reversal in the
Supreme Court of Florida was limited to the
State's assignments of error concerning only
that ground covered in the final decree of the
chancellor. Thus, there are questions of
constitutionality which have not yet been
decided by the courts. The serious question
of the meaning of contributions of any nature
was not decided in this case by the Supreme
Court of Florida.

The procedurally limited nature of opinions
rendered subsequent to the decision of the
trial court has narrowed some issues and
excluded consideration of others. It is
respectfully suggested therefore that in the
event this Court declines to decide questions
raised at trial but not considered by the
Supreme Court of Florida that the cause be
remanded to afford the Florida court that
opportunity. In that way Appellant will not
be penalized for having convinced the trial
court and thereby precluding his need to
assign error. It is respectfully urged,
however, that pursuant to Epperson, supra,
this Court should decide the questions
raised by appeal.

CONCLUSION

It is respectfully submitted that Petition
for Rehearing should be granted.

MILTON E. GRUSMARK and
NATALIE BASKIN

By_____
      Natalie Baskin

I HEREBY CERTIFY that a true and correct copy of the foregoing Petition for Rehearing of Dismissal of Appeal was mailed to Earl Faircloth, Attorney General and Robert Chasta Assistant Attorney General, Attorneys for Appellees, The Capitol, Tallahassee, Florida 32304, this____ day of February, 1969.

MILTON E. GRUSMARK and
NATALIE BASKIN
Attorneys for Appellant
1674 Meridian Avenue
Miami Beach, Florida 33

By_____
     Natalie Baskin

SUPREME COURT OF THE UNITED STATES

October Term, 1968.

SUTTON, ETC *v.* ADAMS, SECRETARY OF STATE OF FLORIDA, ET AL.

APPEAL FROM THE SUPREME COURT OF FLORIDA.

No. 726. Decided January 20, 1969.

PER CURIAM.

The appeal is dismissed for want of a substantial federal question.

MR. JUSTICE BLACK and MR. JUSTICE HARLAN would note probable jurisdiction and set the case for oral argument.

APPENDIX A

I HEREBY CERTIFY that the foregoing
Petition for Rehearing is presented in good
faith and not for delay.

MILTON E. GRUSMARK and
NATALIE BASKIN

By_____

APPENDIX B

CPSIA information can be obtained
at www.ICGtesting.com
Printed in the USA
BVHW012023281221
625072BV00012B/540

9 781270 6229